The Family *of* Adoption

Joyce Maguire Pavao

Beacon Press
Boston

Beacon Press
25 Beacon Street
Boston, Massachusetts 02108-2892
www.beacon.org

Beacon Press books
are published under the auspices of
the Unitarian Universalist Association of Congregations.

"See One Face" by Sylvia Ramos Leary reprinted by permission of the author.
"My Dog Story," "Responding to a Poem by Mi Ok Bruining," and "Daddy" from
An Adoptee's Dreams by Penny Callan Partridge (Bethesda, Md.: Gateway Press, 1995).
Copyright 1995 by Penny Callan Partridge. Reprinted by permission of the author.
"From a Daughter's Perspective" by Kelley McGee reprinted by permission of the author.

09 08 07 06 05   8 7 6 5 4 3 2 1

This book is printed on acid-free paper that meets the uncoated paper
ANSI / NISO specifications for permanence as revised in 1992.

Text design by John Kane
Composition by Wilsted & Taylor Publishing Services

Library of Congress Cataloging-in-Publication Data

Pavao, Joyce Maguire.
    The family of adoption / Joyce Maguire Pavao.
       p.   cm.
    ISBN 0-8070-2827-4
    1. Adoption.   2. Family.   3. Adopted children—Family relationships.
    4. Adoptees—Family relationships.   5. Adoptive parents.   6. Birthparents.
    I. Title.
    HV875.P38   1998
    362. 73′4—dc21   97–52346

To my two mothers,
and especially to my daughter, Seacia Scheherazade Pavao,
who has taught me
much of what I know about connections and family

Contents

ix Preface

1 Chapter 1
   Parental rites: The birth parent

21 Chapter 2
   Parental rites: The adoptive parent

40 Chapter 3
   The adopted child, birth to eight years

54 Chapter 4
   The adopted preadolescent (eight to twelve years) and early adolescent (twelve to sixteen years)

75 Chapter 5
   The adopted adolescent and young adult

93 Chapter 6
   Keeping connections

115 Epilogue
   Adoption and beyond

131 Adoption glossary

143 Acknowledgments

Preface

A young teenaged girl kept a huge secret. She never told her boyfriend. She never told her best friend. She never told her mother. She was pregnant. The day of the birth, she had "cramps" and her six-year-old sister was sent to get help because they thought she had appendicitis. I am the appendix. I am the secret.

The girl's mother, given only a few hours' notice, was not prepared or willing to be involved with this (this being me).

Secrecy was first, but love had grown alongside it. The teenager had come to love her secret and had fantasies of keeping the child. She was devastated when her mother would not help. She had to continue to live in secrecy after her baby was gone. No one could know.

There was a couple who had been married for many years and were quite happy. The husband was a young, up-and-coming businessman. They had a beautiful home. They had summers by the shore and friends and family galore. After the pain of infertility, they had adopted one child, who was now six, and they wanted another. They adopted the teenager's baby.

In those days the process was all secret. They were told very little about the teenager; she was told close to nothing about them.

The baby was given a new name. The smells, the sounds around her changed. She was adaptive and she grew. She was loved and cared for. There was no lack of material things. There was appreciation of her and love for her, but somehow there was no essential acknowledgment of who she was.

The baby-turned-child was curious. Her red hair was blamed for her feistiness and temper and her irrepressible curiosity. She asked questions constantly about everything, but especially about herself. Who was she? Her parents read to her and answered her questions . . . except those about herself and except those about her adoption.

When she asked those questions, her mother, in particular, would get a sad and distant look and would change the subject. That was the worst thing you could do to the red-haired girl who appreciated honesty and directness and hated secrets. If people didn't answer, was it a secret? She was, of course, told that she was adopted. But only once—and no child can take in something this important and complicated after hearing it only once.

A mean child in the neighborhood taunted the red-haired girl as she rollerskated one day. "Ha, ha, you're adopted. You have red hair and you don't look like anyone in your family . . . ha, ha." The red-haired girl went crying home to her mother and told her what the girl had said. Her mother said, "Red hair is a recessive gene. Tell Carol to drop dead." That helped, to tell Carol, with her hands on her hips, armed with good vocabulary like "recessive." Carol backed off, but the red-haired girl was well aware that her mother had not addressed the issue of adoption. She knew she was adopted and she knew it must be a very bad thing, because no one would talk about it except to tease her.

Throughout her childhood, neighbors and relatives made comments about adoption, but no one taught the red-haired girl how to respond. Just as her birth mother had dealt with her pregnancy alone and kept silent, her adoptive parents were keeping the secret of infertility and could not talk about adoption easily, if at all.

The red-haired girl turned into a teenager. She was very smart and social in high school. She wanted to be included. She hung out with the wrong crowd and missed curfews. It was safer to come in late and be punished by her parents (who loved her but seemed unreasonable) than to be excluded by her friends.

✢

The baby, the red-haired child, is, of course, me. Adoption has shaped my life from the moment my maternal birth grandmother entered the hospital and recovered from the shock that her daughter had concealed a pregnancy and given birth.

Adoption has shaped my life through the loss my birth mother experienced and through the losses my adoptive parents experienced. It shaped my life as I tried as a child, all alone, to figure it out while no one would talk, no one would explain.

It shaped my life throughout a terribly difficult adolescence, as I yearned to please my parents but needed even more to please—to know—myself.

One of the things that was most healing was my search for my birth mother. Her life had been shaped by secrecy as well. She married rather quickly and had six boys and a girl. We created a good relationship, but due to her shame and her need for continued secrecy, it was constrained. She was greatly relieved to know that I was all right though, and we had a very intense time every time we met or talked on the phone.

My mothers died six weeks apart. They both died of secrecy. One could no longer talk, silenced by her disease. One could no longer think or remember. Both of my mothers are together now. I have no more divided loyalty. I love and cherish what each set of parents gave to me, and especially what each of my mothers endured and imparted. I regret that they were not allowed to be whole and I celebrate that I am whole. I refuse to have secrets and I work to change a system that perpetuates them.

My bias shows. I am most interested in the best interest of the baby and child, not for just one moment in time, but for all the moments of that child's lifetime. Adoption is not an event. Adoption is not a snapshot in time. It is a moving picture that goes on through this life and into the ones that follow.

As a family-systems thinker, I cannot forget the importance of understanding all of the parents, birth and adoptive, and their needs and concerns as well. It is quite important to look at these complex families as a system and to see the adults' needs clearly and compassionately, since their impact on the life of the adopted child is so profound.

Today's adoptions are quite different from mine. Clearly, there is more openness in adoption in general. People talk about, write about, and think about all that adoption means, and in many cases—even in international adoptions—parents *can* have more information about their children. If we are entrusting a child to adoptive parents, shouldn't we also entrust all of the child's information to those parents?

Today's adoptive parents can travel to the child's country or state of origin. They are able to understand more about the culture and family that the child is from, and about the beginnings of the child's life. It is more common for adoptive parents and birth parents to meet—if only once—so that they are able to see the other mother and/or father who is connected to this child whom they both love. Times change, politics change, technologies change, and more and more we are able to find information readily.

Even in the case of international adoptions—where we used to think that it was impossible to find the family of origin—today's families are more often finding the information that they need, and sometimes even meeting the family of origin when the child is still young. Access to information is improving all the time. Adopted people from China, for instance, may not have access to their information today, but may have in the years to come.

One adoptive parent I know, an Italian woman named Anna, searched the world to find out what she could do to be the best parent to her children, who were adopted from Russia. She often attends adoption conferences in the United States. She tells me that "in Italy people do not talk about connections in adoption. Italy is perhaps like the U.S. was twenty or more years ago, and people still try to pretend as if the children of adoption are born into their adoptive families."

It is Anna's heartfelt caring for the previous life of her daughter, Dasha, that led her to take Dasha on a pilgrimage to her town of origin in Russia. It was there—walking with Dasha, and seeing the place where her daughter began her life, seeing the orphanage where she lived until she was adopted, seeing the grave of her first mother—that Anna felt that she had finally, and truly, come together with her daughter, through this respect for and acknowledgement of who Dasha was before her life in her present family, and in Italy, began.

It is not easy to take risks when one's life has been marked by loss. So many adoptive parents have experienced the losses of infertility. When Anna took the risk of revisiting the past life of her daughter, Dasha, she did not know what they would each find. She did not know how it would affect Dasha, or how it would affect her. She did not know how it would affect their relationship with each other. But in the end, she states, "It has given me more of my daughter." What a gift for each of them: to be able to weave the past into the present, in order to create a fully integrated future for their whole extended family of adoption.

We have learned through the voices of adults adopted thirty, forty, fifty years ago, that not having access to certain facts and information about oneself can be harmful to the adopted individual. This lack of respect for the adopted person's origins and past dishonors and disrespects the reality of his/her life. It does not give the adopted person the information that can help him/her to search and find the place within his/her heart and soul where he/she can integrate the past and the present, in order to have a future.

✛

The Family of Adoption is meant, then, for everyone in the world of adoption. My hope is that it will give a broad framework within which to think about adoption as a whole system, so that everyone involved will learn to feel some empathy for the other members of the adoption world and will thereby grow and heal themselves. It is meant for birth parents and their families, for preadoptive parents and their families, and for the families who are living in adoption. It is meant for the siblings who are born into a family and share that family with adopted siblings, for the spouses of people who are adopters, adopted people, or birth parents. And it is meant for the children of all of the above. Adoption issues affect generations before and the generations that follow as well. It is also meant for the professionals who work with the people who live in adoption—the doctors, nurses, midwives, lawyers, judges, clergy, social workers, psychologists, family therapists, and teachers. Without the understanding and help of a larger community, the challenges for these families are that much greater.

One wonderful change that has happened in the last fifteen years is the amount of media focusing on adoption, especially the availability of books and articles about adoption. Adoptive parents today are, for the most part, well educated. There are adoptive parents who read everything they can find on the subject, who attend conferences, and who learn that they have a right to have more information about the child they will parent and love forever.

Over the past thirty years, as I've worked in the field of family therapy and adoption, I've found the way to integrate my personal, professional, and political beliefs concerning the family of adoption. I have developed models for the treatment of adoptive families which have been universalized to be used with foster care, guardianship, kinship, divorce, and other blended families. I have also developed models for training the professionals who work with these families.

I have had the honor and the privilege to work with many resilient, respectful, resourceful, and rejoicing families created through adoption. Those families and their stories have inseparably informed the work I have done in my field and they are everywhere present in this book. I am thrilled that I have been an educator—not only for those who live and work in the world of adoption, and know firsthand how unique the family of adoption is, but also for those other people in the world who constantly interface with us, but have no idea at all about what adoption really is in today's world.

Over thirty years ago, when there were no adoption services other than those attached to adoption agencies, and when no one considered the postadoption needs of families, I founded the Adoption Resource Center (ARC) to address them. Over twenty years ago, I founded and developed the Pre/post Adoption Consulting Team (PACT), and ten years ago I established Family Connections Training (FACT) Institute. All of these programs are now under one nonprofit umbrella called the Center for Family Connections (CFFC) in Cambridge, Massachusetts, and in New York City.

One of the unusual things about the PACT team at Center for Family Connections is that it is not related to the "business" of adoption: it is not part of an adoption agency and does not place infants or children for adoption. It was conscientiously designed to be free-standing. Many of the adoptive parents that we see are reluctant to go back to the agency or office where they adopted their child: after all, they were carefully scrutinized to see if they were good enough parents and they fear that admitting to difficulty proves that they aren't. Many adoptees find it hard to go to the place where they were adopted from, and many birth parents are unable to return to the last place they saw or held their child. These people do not seek the services of that agency or place even though it does, in fact, have a great deal of information and expertise about adoption.

We serve birth parents who are placing children for adoption, who have had children removed and their parental rights terminated, or who have had a child placed in adoption in the past. We serve preadoptive couples and individuals who are thinking about adoption, and we serve intergenerational families, including the extended families of the preadoptive couple or individual, the extended family of the birth mother and birth father and their subsequent families, and adult adopted people and their own subsequent families—a wide range of people, all with adoption-related issues.

We also do training and consulting in the areas of adoption, foster care, guardianship, kinship, and divorce, and work with gay and lesbian parents, single parents, and parents who have conceived a child with a donor's egg or sperm. The common factor in all of these families is their complexity and the resulting need to clarify each person's roles and responsibilities, as well as the need to learn how and when to talk to the children about these complex issues that are a very real part of their lives.

Underlying all of our work is the belief that in order to work with adoptive and other complex families, it is important to have a sense of the family as a whole and to understand the role of what I've called "normative crises in the development of the adoptive family." "Normative crises" may sound somewhat anomalous. Crises are in fact normal at many life stages. Crises are not always bad. They often occur at junctures in life, or during times of change and transition. In adoption, there are several classic crises that occur in many families, and I have worked to educate professionals and families so they understand that these situations are normal given the circumstances of adoption: because the ways in which these crises are responded to, by both parents and professionals, has a large impact on what happens within any given family at any juncture. I describe "normative crises" throughout *The Family of Adoption*.

But I have come to believe very strongly that birth and adoptive families are not the only ones responsible for the family of adoption. There are very few professionals who have had any training about adoption and its impact on individuals and families. Once, after I gave an address to the American Academy of Pediatrics, a physician told me he had searched for material on adoption in medical school texts and had found only one page with three little paragraphs. Three paragraphs are all that our child psychiatrists, pediatricians, obstetricians, gynecologists, and general practitioners are taught about adoption, unless they choose to seek that education on their own. Law schools, also, have neglected to give our lawyers and judges a broader framework within which to view adoption and serve each client and case.

In social work programs, there is sometimes a case presentation involving foster care or adoption, but it is rare to get the training that would be most helpful to prepare social workers to work with these complex families. Most psychology programs do not have professors who know about adoption. Candidates interested in working in this field are very often without knowledgeable professors on their reviewing committees. Even so, it is heartening that we are seeing more and more dissertations being written about adoption and related matters. The writing and research on adoption has, in fact, tripled in the last fifteen years.

There are too few well-trained professionals available to do the preadoptive consulting and educating that would help birth parents and adoptive parents before they embark on the adoption course. The first person that someone seeking information encounters is usually someone representing an agency, and the counseling that's available is constrained by the work of the agency. More and more we are finding that adoptions in the nation are not based on a consideration of the child's welfare but on business considerations. This is a sad change of events.

Our professional schools need to add curriculum that will provide the training necessary to work with these families in a way that does not pathologize, but rather supports and guides them through the normal challenges of being an adoptive family. It is my hope that people in law schools, medical schools, public health schools, schools of social work and of psychology and family therapy, divinity schools, and schools of education will use *The Family of Adoption* to understand adoption in a larger, more systemic way and with a developmental and intergenerational perspective.

I hope in this way all of these professionals will become better prepared to understand the needs of the clients and patients they serve in the world of adoption.

When adoption is done ethically, when it is the right thing for all of the parents, birth and adoptive, when the extended families have been educated and worked with and when the community is well prepared, then we all know we have expanded our lives, expanded our families, and expanded our hearts.

Chapter 1
Parental rites: The birth parent

There have always been mothers and fathers who have not been able to, or not chosen to, or not been allowed to, parent their children, whether because of substance abuse, war, poverty, youth, scarcity, illness, or coercion. Not all mothers and fathers are parents, and not all parents give birth to the children that they raise. This is how it has always been and how it will always be.

It makes sense to place birth parents at the beginning of any dialogue about the system of adoption, since that is where much of the story of adoption begins. But language, we have learned, is an equally important starting point: we can't expect any adoption to begin on a healthy basis when parental roles and relationships are badly defined and named. In the past, birth parents were sometimes referred to as "biological parents." This made many feel angry, as if they were being referred to as "baby machines" without feelings, as if their involvement had been reduced simply to a physiological process. This is not how most mothers and fathers who conceive and produce a child feel, and it is an equally harmful and painful message to convey to an adopted child.

Sometimes, birth parents are referred to as the "real" or the "natural" parents. This understandably makes the adoptive parents feel discounted. It confuses the child and makes him or her wonder which parents are "real."

The truth is that both sets of parents are "real." During the developmental stages of early childhood, when a child's thinking is concrete, an adopted child needs to understand that there *are* two mothers and two fathers, but there is only one set of, or one *parent*. The role of *parent* must be made clear and distinguished from that of mother and father.

A child, after all, clearly understands that there can be many mothers and fathers. People may have multiple grandmothers and grandfathers, a godmother and godfather, a stepmother or stepfather—and they may also have a birth mother and birth father. In all adoptions, legal and emotional, it is the *roles,* not the labels, that must be most carefully defined for the child.

In a kinship adoption, for instance, if a grandparent is parenting the child, the clarification of responsibilities is even more important. The fact that the child's birth mother is in the role of "sister" or "aunt" and that the grandmother is the "mother," as in *parent,* should be explained and made clear so that it does not come as a surprise or feel like a lie for the child at a later age. When a child's trust is ruined because of lies or miscommunication about these roles it causes lasting trauma for the child and ultimately for the whole family.

The terminology, then, is extremely important. Although this is not perfect, over the years people involved with adoption have developed a vocabulary that feels most comfortable for everyone. We use "birth mother and birth father" to describe the parents who gave birth to the child, or the root parents; "adoptive parents" is the preferred term for the parents adopting and raising the child.

People don't usually add adjectives when speaking to each other, of course, but rather, when it is necessary to refer to each set of parents or children to avoid confusion. I never referred to my adoptive parents as my "adoptive parents"; they were always "my parents," unless I was telling a story that included both my birth and adoptive parents and I needed to clarify which set I was referring to. I have always addressed my birth mother as "Eileen." I did not know her until I was in my twenties, and although she is my "mother," the person who gave birth to me, our relationship, the roles we had in each other's lives, were profoundly influenced by the fact that she had never been my parent. When I first met Eileen, I was grappling with the divided loyalty that adopted people have at various stages of development, and I simply felt most comfortable calling her by her first name. When I am speaking *of* her, I call her my birth mother—the mother who gave me birth and life.

There are many different kinds of adoptions and many ways in which a child is surrendered by birth parents to adoptive parents. Most people think of adoption only as what *they* know it to be. If you adopted an infant or if you were adopted as an infant, you usually think of this version as adoption. If you were involved in a foster-adoption, you think this is what adoption is. If yours is an international or transracial adoption, you may be basing all of your thoughts about adoption on that particular experience. If your child or children were removed from your care due to abuse or neglect, you may think of that kind of removal and placement as adoption.

In all of these kinds of adoptions the experience of the birth parents involved will be different in some ways. In order to begin to talk about the birth parents' experience with adoption, though, I've chosen one broad-brush scenario: that of a young woman who has become pregnant accidentally, has been referred to us, and has a very difficult decision to make.

The referrals that we get in these cases are from obstetricians, clinics, and adoption agencies. The private and public mental health agencies in the area also send birth parents to us for family therapy, because the decision is a serious one that has an impact upon many lives.

The first step in my family consultation model is to involve the birth mother's family (and the birth father's when possible) in family therapy. Both birth parents need to take time to understand that the decision they are making is a lifelong one, and their families, whenever this is possible, need to understand and support this decision. If this can be done, there is little chance of a change of mind down the road, or of finding out after the fact that a family member wants the child after he or she has already begun to attach to a preadoptive family.

For many of these young people, for the birth mother especially, there are huge pressures: pressures from family; pressures based on fears or based on truths; pressures communicated by the agency or the social worker; pressures from society. With all of these pressures, the decision to place a child is a terribly hard one to make, in part because it requires abstract thinking about what giving up this child actually will be like, not just now, but forever. The decision to parent—often to parent alone—requires equally abstract thinking at this stage. And either decision will last a lifetime and affect many lives.

Most people who have to make this very difficult decision about whether or not to place a child for adoption have never really thought about adoption before. They need to sort through the realities of being a single parent; the availability of support if they choose to raise the child on their own; the possibility of having a member of the extended family raise the child.

Although I am focusing here on young birth parents, many of

whom are poor or do not have a family or community network to support them, it is important to remember that some birth parents considering adoption are older. Many these days are already raising a child or children and know, concretely, that they cannot afford or care for another child. A very large number of today's birth parents are married couples suffering from poverty and loss of jobs who, in trying to keep together the family they already have, make the decision to place a second or third child for adoption. Some birth parents facing adoption have had their children removed because of neglect or abuse and, after a period of time, either agree or are forced by the courts and public agencies to sign a "termination of parental rights" so that the children have a permanent home rather than a temporary foster placement.

We have learned that it is clearly not in the best interest of the child to be moved from birth family to foster family to adoptive family. The fewer moves the better for the infant or child. Experts all agree that this is so, and yet our public welfare system has shuffled children (some, appallingly, as many as sixteen times in five years). By constantly moving children after long periods when attachment is underway, we are creating children who will be emotionally cut off and not able to attach.

It is clear that in many older-child adoptions, the birth parents' ambivalence toward adoption and a child's real or imaginary belief that he or she was "taken" is a primary cause of disrupted adoptions. The "termination of parental rights" document is in need of reworking. We do need to have the parents who cannot parent surrender the full right of parenting to a permanent family, but the wording also suggests that they cut off all emotional and psychological ties as well. Many birth parents are willing to leave children in foster care, or even in guardianship, rather than sign a legal document that says that they give up all attachment and connection.

We have been mediating guardianship or open adoption agreements with parents that cannot parent for the past twenty years and it is a successful procedure for all involved—most especially the children.

Many birth parents are predominantly clear about their decision to place a child for adoption. Some, however, are extremely ambivalent about this choice.

My own feeling—and it is backed up by practice with this model over time—is that when a young birth mother is extremely ambivalent, it is invaluable to place her either with her own family, if they are available and supportive, or with a fostering family who will act as a holding environment for her while she parents the infant. Then she can make a fully informed and concrete decision whether or not to place her baby for adoption. It is not easy to find foster homes for both an adolescent and an infant, but we have worked hard to develop a network of these homes. We work closely with the foster family or with the birth parents' families, if they will cooperate in this way, to give the birth mother an opportunity to experience, concretely, what it is like to parent her baby seven days a week, twenty-four hours a day, and to make a decision concerning her own and her child's future that is based on reality, not on abstract thinking.

This plan helps everyone in the long run, because when the decision is made, it is a conscious and clear one. There has been time to work with the extended family, and, if supports are there, they have emerged before, not after, a preadoptive family has begun to attach to the baby or even to the idea of this particular baby. The adoptive parents benefit as well because there has been no unnecessary disruption for the infant— there has been only one placement.

Even so, most agencies and adoptive parents fear this approach will mean fewer babies being placed for adoption. They worry that if given this kind of time for consideration, the birth parents or birth families will decide to keep the child within the family. I believe strongly that when the adoption is truly the plan of all parties involved, when it is done conscientiously and with compassion, it has a greater rate of life-long success. There would be fewer contested adoptions and fewer situations of loss for preadoptive parents (who have already suffered enough loss) if we made sure that each and every adoption is truly the right decision. Birth and adoptive parents aside, it is the *child* who is at greater risk when we do not do conscientious adoption planning.

The act of adoption is often centered around the crises of the adults—the untimely pregnancy or the removal of a child for abuse or neglect for the birth parent, the infertility or desire to increase one's family through adoption for the preadoptive parents. Rarely do we truly think about the trauma to the baby or child that happens in the process of what ends in adoption. If adoption were truly child-centered—about finding families for children—we would be working very hard to prevent attachment problems and to provide transitions that are kind and loving for the infant or child.

⊹

Stories are a tool I use over and over again in thinking and teaching about adoption, because I believe we learn best when we are moved intellectually *and* emotionally. All of the stories in this book reflect those of people I have seen therapeutically over twenty-five years, with names and other information altered and merged. I've been challenged in the past over the fact that, since we provide clinical services, our clients may not be a representative sampling of what happens in adoption. Of course, any sampling is just that—a sampling.

My orientation in therapy, though, is one of strength and health, not of pathology. Not all of the clients we see at our clinic are there for "therapy."

Many come for adoption education or for a consultation or even a little coaching about what to do in a difficult situation when they don't have abundant role models of other families in the same boat. Although our clients—and their stories as they appear in this book—might be seen as coming from a "clinical population," I believe they represent a true and rich range of adoption experiences.

Susan's story   A young woman named Susan came to see me almost fourteen years ago. She was seventeen years old and had been referred by her obstetrician. Susan was seven months pregnant. She was, from the beginning, clear that she was going to give birth to this baby. Abortion was not a choice for her. And yet, she was having a great deal of trouble deciding whether she would be able to keep her child and become a parent, or whether she should begin to plan for an adoption.

Susan's parents were alcoholics and they had abused her. She was the oldest and "parentified" child with three younger siblings. Susan had run away from home when she was almost sixteen years old and ended up in a halfway house. She was receiving counseling there and trying to get her life in order when she became pregnant. She knew only the first name of the birth father and never saw him again after the night they spent together.

Susan felt as if she were about to gain some control over her life, and now *this* was happening to her.

Since her parents lived in another state and were still active alcoholics, she felt distanced from them and refused to involve them in the counseling. Although the counselor from the halfway house tried to help Susan find the birth father, she couldn't locate him, and so neither he nor his family were available as Susan was trying to make her decision.

I asked that she bring her counselor in for our sessions. First we talked about what it would be like to be a single parent. I asked Susan and her counselor to visit a high school that had a program for parenting teens, and to go to the Department of Social Services to see what kinds of support—services and housing—she might receive to help raise her child. Then we started to talk about the alternative: adoption. We talked about what adoption is and what it means.

Susan was surprised to learn that she might be able to meet the preadoptive couple or individual, and that she might also have some choice as to what kind of family her child would belong to and be raised in.

The due date was coming up quickly, though, and Susan was still totally ambivalent. I believed that we would be making a huge mistake to push this young pregnant woman to make a decision prior to the birth, or at the moment of the birth. So, Susan's baby girl was born, and she chose to go from the hospital with her baby to a foster home.

It is very painful to watch preadoptive parents who take a high-risk placement, one where the birth mother is as ambivalent as Susan was, and then to see the birth mother decide that she wishes to keep the child.

And, it is not in the best interest of a child, even an infant, to have things as unsettled and tense as they always are in a contested adoption situation. For these reasons, I feel it makes far more sense to make sure that the birth parents and their families, as much as possible, are over the greater ambivalence about the adoption decision and, therefore, able to make the right and permanent decision.

The foster family with whom Susan and her baby were placed worked hard not to "parent" her child, so that Susan could have a concrete education on what it meant to take care of her baby twenty-four hours a day, seven days a week. Susan soon found that her life was changed radically; that she could not be the adolescent that she had been before the pregnancy and birth of her child. This was very hard for Susan; she had lost her childhood to her parents' alcoholism, and she felt as if she was about to lose her adolescence as well.

Within six weeks of her baby's birth, Susan made the painful decision to place her child for adoption. She had matured and had truly bonded with this baby whom she loved very much. Yet, she felt that for the sake of her own life and for the baby's, she needed to plan for adoption. One of the major influences in her decision was that she didn't feel she had enough resources to make it on her own. She feared she might have to return to her parents' home, and she did not want her childhood experience to be repeated for her newborn daughter. Susan realized in the end that she was not ready to be a parent even though she was now a mother.

Susan decided to work with an agency that had a semi-open adoption policy. She wanted to meet the preadoptive couple and to have them meet her.

She wanted a family without a history of alcoholism—a family that loved children and would respect and raise her child with strong values.

I remember the day she met the couple who might parent her child. Susan asked me to come with her. She was very frightened. She was afraid that the couple wouldn't like her. We talked a great deal about her fears and insecurities regarding them, and about the fact that the couple were probably feeling fearful that she wouldn't like *them*—that they really wanted a baby and were afraid that she wouldn't think they were good enough. All parties are fragile and fearful of being rejected, of not being respected at this particularly vulnerable point in the adoption process.

We arrived at the agency, and what happened next was very moving. Susan clearly loved her baby. She told the story of how this untimely pregnancy had come about, and why she was placing the child for adoption, and what she wanted in a family for this child. The preadoptive couple told how on their third date they knew that they loved each other and would marry and how they'd talked about the family they would have, the number of children and their names. They talked about how hard it had been for them to deal with infertility, and that the bottom line was that they wanted to be parents and were ready to be parents.

They cried (along with, by then, everyone else in the room) and said that they would love the honor of parenting Susan's child.

There was a respect that you could feel between the preadoptive couple and the birth mother. Later, in the chapter on adolescent issues, it will become clear just how important it is that the child receive a positive image and positive messages about the birth parent from the adoptive parents—how important for the identity development and self-esteem of that child. This couple clearly had a very positive feeling about Susan at the meeting. The child was placed with them for adoption.

This was the first semi-open adoption for that particular agency, and they were nervous about it. Only first names were mentioned in this meeting, and the agreement with the agency was that Susan and the adoptive couple could exchange letters annually and that the agency would only pass on non-identifying information between the families.

About eighteen months after Susan had placed her daughter, Krista, for adoption, I had a telephone call in the middle of the night from her. She had had a dream that her baby had died, and she felt she had killed her baby by giving her away. She felt that there was no point in her living and she was clearly suicidal.

After a great deal of talking and calming her down, I got Susan to promise to come in the next morning. In my office, in the morning, I was able to call the agency and to ask them if the child Susan had delivered and loved was alive and healthy.

Susan needed to have concrete information about that child then; it was a life and death situation for her. This would never have been possible in the past, because in a closed adoption there was no way for a birth parent to do anything but fantasize. In this case, the social worker we had worked with was able to get in touch with the adoptive parents. They were more than happy to give some information, and the information was very positive: the baby was brilliant and wonderful, walking and talking, and they were so proud of her. They would send a picture to Susan. This information actually saved Susan's life. She kept that picture of her little girl on her desk at work and told people it was her niece, Krista. She decided it was not the business of her colleagues to know about her past and she was not willing to tell her intimate story to acquaintances, so she made up this small lie. That photograph and what it symbolizes has been important and life-sustaining for Susan in the midst of her loss.

Every year, around the time of Emily's birthday (Emily is Susan's daughter's new name—and the middle name that Susan had given to Krista at birth), the adoptive family writes a letter explaining what the baby is doing and telling Susan funny anecdotes about her. The "baby" will be thirteen this year. Susan writes, too, almost every year, and tells them something about herself. Susan often feels saddest about the loss of her daughter at Emily's birthday, which sometimes makes her unable to write and send a photo. These feelings for birth parents, at the time of their child's birthday, are nearly universal. Anniversary dates often bring up memories, especially for people who are grieving. For the birth mother the grieving process is lifelong, even when her decision was conscious and informed—the best decision she could make—and remains that way. There is grief over the loss of a child that lingers, no matter what the circumstances.

The stages birth parents go through are very real and need to be understood. Many adoptive parents who make plans for some open contact through letters, etc., are gravely disappointed and feel betrayed when the birth mother does not write back. It may be that it is too painful for the birth mother at that particular time and that, like Susan, she can't always respond on schedule.

The initial period of grieving lasts roughly five to seven years. Remember that for the birth parents there are no rites of passage and no ceremonies that include one's friends and family, that gather around them in the grieving process. For the most part their grieving is done alone. And this is true in open, semi-open, and closed adoptions. The best thing adoptive parents who hope for contact can do is to keep the lines of communication open. Adoptive parents are wise to continue sending letters and pictures, even if there is no response at the moment.

Many birth parents spend the early period, after the surrender, as do people who have other kinds of posttraumatic stress. There is a period of emotional moratorium, and often there is no interest in opening up the intense pain of the initial loss, even in the planned open adoptions that are being done more frequently these days. In some instances, the adoptive parents understand the need for connections and are trying to make the relationship more open while the birth parents are holding back. This can be frustrating if adoptive parents do not know that this period of separation is a normal part of healing rites for many birth parents.

Susan came in for couples therapy with David, her fiance, at one point. She wanted him to understand that she was a mother even though her daughter didn't live with her—even though she wasn't a parent. She didn't want any of this to be a secret. She wanted David to understand why she becomes sad after they visit his sister and her husband who have a child the same age as Emily. She wanted David to read the letters she receives through the agency, and she wanted to keep the pictures out in her house so that she could feel open about the child that she is not raising. She did an excellent job of educating David about who she is and what this all means to her.

When David and Susan eventually married, Susan was very nervous, as many birth parents are, about having another child, the "second first child," who would replace the child who was lost. Sometimes birth mothers make a quick move to replace the child, and sometimes there's a fear that keeps them from *ever* having another child. They often feel terribly guilty about keeping the second first child when they were not able to keep the first.

What if Emily's adoptive parents had never met Susan? What if all that they knew of her was that she was a runaway, age seventeen, currently living in a halfway house; that she was the abused child of alcoholic parents; that the birth father was unknown, their baby conceived on a one-night stand.

What if they had not met Susan and all that they knew of her was from the notes taken by a social worker—the truth, but not all of who Susan is. What the adoptive parents know about the birth mother inevitably affects their thinking, and therefore the adopted child's.

Claire's story   I once worked with a woman who had surrendered a child seventeen years before. Claire came from a very wealthy white family. Her parents sent her off to college, and during her first year she became pregnant by her African-American boyfriend. Not only were her parents horrified that she was pregnant, but the fact that she was going to have a biracial child was extremely upsetting to them. Claire's father was on the board of a private mental hospital. He made arrangements for Claire to be placed in this hospital for the remaining months of her pregnancy, and the parents told their friends that Claire had had a nervous breakdown under the pressures of college.

Years later, when I saw her in therapy, Claire told me that her psychiatrist in the mental hospital had kept telling her, "You're not crazy, your family is. But we have to keep you here because of your father's position and power."

Even so, it was difficult to be alone and pregnant for those several months and to wonder what was going to happen. After the placement of her child, which was arranged by her parents, Claire was not able to deal with returning to her previous college life, and spent time—understandably—acting out and getting herself into all kinds of trouble.

Eventually she did finish college, began work as a photographer, which she loved, and later married.

Seventeen years later, Claire came to see me at the Adoption Resource Center (ARC), one of the clinics that I had started in the late seventies. She had come, she said, because of her depression for which she had been medicated off and on for many years. Claire felt concerned about how little change there had been in her underlying problems, but she made no mention of adoption. This struck me immediately, because our center was clearly all about adoption; it would be almost impossible to come there and not know that that is what you are coming about, directly or indirectly.

We talked about her personal history, her medical history, we talked about her family history, we did genograms, and after she'd mentioned the long-ago adoption, we talked about the fact that—as is true for many birth parents—depression can be associated with unresolved grief over the loss of a baby to adoption.

At the death of an infant, there is a funeral, and people are sympathetic and empathetic. All religions have rites of passage to mourn the loss of a child when it is through death and the mourning is a shared experience. But there are no rites that accompany the placement of a child. It is very hard for a birth mother to get the kind of empathy she needs, often even from a therapist. Claire had not received any help confronting or resolving her loss.

Claire had joined a grass-roots organization called Concerned United Birth Parents (CUB), which is a group that provides support for birth parents. This led her to realize that people actually searched for, and found out, what had happened to the child they had placed years before. Claire was frightened, but also galvanized, by one story she'd heard at a CUB meeting. Another birth mother, who had searched for her son, found that he had never been adopted. He had fallen between the cracks and ended up in the foster care system for years. This enraged the woman because she had been told, "You are a single woman in college. You can't parent this child, and we will provide a two-parent family"; her social worker had assured her that the adoption plan she had agreed to was in the best interest of her child. It is nearly always possible for people to trace someone if they have enough money and/or the right connections. Claire was able to find out, with the help of a private detective, where her son was living, where he was at school, and what the adoptive family's background and life was like. She was not interested in disrupting the family in any way, however, or in doing anything that would hurt her son or his family.

She was simply interested in knowing that he was all right. Since he had been adopted out of a mental hospital, her biggest fear was that if he had acted out when he was five or six his parents might have assumed he was schizophrenic. How had his parents reacted to their knowledge that he came from a mental hospital?

What if he chose to search for his birth parents when he turned eighteen (the age at which grass-roots organizations will help someone search without their adoptive parents' involvement) and discovered he was born in a mental hospital? Would he go any further? Would he make assumptions about his background, knowing that his mother had been in a mental hospital?

Claire was extremely careful with her search, and she did an interesting thing. She subscribed to the newspaper of the town where her son lived. Over time, Claire would come rushing into an appointment waving a newspaper in her hand saying, "I have something to show you," and there would be the high school football team from her son's hometown. There were all these little helmeted heads, so you could barely make out the faces, but underneath was his name—his adoptive name. She said, "He's alive and he has two arms and two legs. He plays football." It was extremely important for her to know that he was okay.

Several months later, she came in to her therapy session waving another newspaper, this time with an article about the spring musical at her birth son's high school. He was to be one of the lead actors. She and her husband flew to the state where he lived, drove to the high school, and sat in the auditorium to watch the musical. She said that she cried through the whole thing. He was fabulous! He was wonderful! His performance and the experience of seeing him was extremely moving to her.

The most important thing (which her husband had to describe to me because she was dissolved in tears) was that during the intermission, they actually saw him with his family and friends. He quite obviously had a very loving family. He seemed well adjusted and had lots of friends. Claire had the answer she had needed for so long: her son had not been irretrievably harmed, had not fallen through the cracks.

The next morning she and her husband drove to the agency that had handled his adoption and asked if they could leave some information in his file.

She wrote a letter, not giving very much information, but simply saying there were some discrepancies in what her birth son might find in the midst of a search. Claire wrote that she wanted to be available to him if he had any questions. She left her address and telephone number in the file. This was more than a few years ago, when agencies were not prone to encourage a search. Many birth mothers, birth fathers, and adoptive parents, as a matter of fact, have discovered that information they'd mailed to their adoption agency or professional to be put in their child's file was not actually placed there—simply because the agency defined its authority broadly enough not to do so.

Claire was luckier. Her birth son, named Ely, waited until he was away at college (the same age that his birth parents had been when he was conceived) to decide that he wanted to search. He went to the agency, was given Claire's letter with her address, and found his birth mother. He and Claire were then able to establish a relationship that was important to both of them. It was crucial to Claire's mental health; she has not taken an antidepressant since that time. Through his connection with Claire, Ely was also able to search for his birth father, with whom she had kept in touch since college. For Ely, a biracial young man raised in a white family, who then found his white birth mother, an integral part of his identity was not available to him until he found his birth father, who was a well-known professor—an excellent role model for Ely who was struggling with college himself.

Sam's story   Several years ago, I received a phone call from a woman named Linda. She was concerned about her father, who she said wasn't sleeping or eating. She felt that he needed to see someone for therapy. She mentioned that she thought this was a unique issue and that I might be able to help.

I asked what had happened.

Three days before, the telephone at her home rang. She picked up one extension, and her eighty-four-year-old father, Sam, who lived in an in-law apartment in the house, picked up another. At the other end of the line was a young woman who wanted to speak with Rose, Sam's wife and Linda's mother, who had been dead for many years. The caller hesitated when she was told this, and then said, "Oh, I'm sorry to hear that." She slowly added, "I'm Rose's granddaughter, and I was looking for her."

Neither Sam nor Linda could understand what she was talking about! They mentally sorted through all the grandchildren, but she was not one of them. And yet, she seemed to know a great deal about Rose. Eventually, the young woman, named Judith, made it clear that her mother had been placed for adoption—by Linda's mother, Sam's wife— and that Judith felt she desperately needed to find this grandmother.

Linda and Sam were confused and disbelieving. Sam asked for Judith's full name and telephone number and said that they would call her back after they had discussed things.

They hung up, turned to one another, and asked, "What was that? Who was she? Was it a lie? Was it a prank?" Sam was very disturbed for several days until he decided to call one of his sisters and said to her, "A strange thing happened to me and I just want to talk to someone. I want to know if you know anything about this." He related the story of Judith's call, and his sister said, "Yes. There was a rumor that Rose had a child and gave up the baby for adoption many years ago, before marrying you."

Sam, who had never been in therapy before, came in with his daughter for our first session. He didn't fully understand why she was bringing him to talk about this. But Sam was a remarkable man. At age eighty-four, his mother and all his siblings were alive, he was self-employed and still worked full time, and he drove his car thirty miles to each of our appointments. His energy and intelligence became a great asset in his therapy.

At our first session he was very angry and he asked, "How could my wife do this to me? It's as if we lived a lie. How could I not have known this about her?" He felt utterly betrayed. Sam asked to be seen alone; it was too difficult for him to talk about all this in front of his daughter.

I often ask clients to bring in photograph albums as a way to talk about the past.

Sam eventually brought in old albums and showed them to me. He would ask, "Does she look happy here? Why does she look happy here if she's holding this information?" "She looks sad here. Shouldn't someone have helped her? Couldn't someone see that she was sad and grieving?" Sam felt distraught because he had not been the one to see any of this and therefore had not been able to help Rose.

I explained what it might have been like to have borne and placed a child for adoption more than forty years ago, and suggested that Rose was probably told *never* to tell anyone, to keep her child a secret. And that she thought she had been doing the only possible thing, the kindest thing, by never telling anyone. He said, "But I was her husband! I was married to her for all those years." I asked if he were angry about her having had sex with another man. Sam was appalled by the question. I told him that he didn't have to talk about it, but that in therapy it was often useful to talk about things that might cause shame or guilt. I asked if he had had lovers before Rose and he said, "Yes, but I was never disloyal to Rose." I added, "The adoption happened before Rose knew you, and she was never disloyal to you. We will never really know what the circumstances are because Rose is not here to tell us."

Eventually Sam's anger dissipated, and he began to experience his sadness. He said many times that Rose should have *told* him. He could have helped her. He said, "The grave spews up secrets. She should have known that I would find out." He talked about how, after the births of each of their four children, Rose was very sad. The doctors all said this was typical—that it was postpartum blues. Slowly, Sam began to see that maybe Rose became depressed because she had lost her first child, and that each subsequent birth brought up the guilt, the shame, and the loss she felt and made her afraid of losing the others.

Something that strongly upset Sam was that ten years earlier— this was according to the granddaughter, Judith—her own mother, Edith, the very child whom Rose had placed for adoption, had telephoned Rose. Edith had searched and discovered where her birth mother was and eventually made the call. But, according to Judith, Rose had said, "I can't talk to you. Nobody knows about this, and I really can't talk to you. Please don't call anymore." Edith, Rose's daughter, respected her wishes. She never called again. Sam now felt though that not only had his wife not told him in the beginning, but even as little as ten years ago she was adding secret to secret.

It was because Judith knew this story and had seen her mother's anguish about never meeting any of her birth family that she had made her own telephone call to Rose's family. We are finding, in our qualitative research at the Center For Family Connections, that many adopted people do not choose to search for their birth families. However, their children often take on the role of searcher and hold many of the adopted person's issues concerning adoptive identity. Just as in many immigrant families in America, the second generation simply wants to be "all-American," to lose the old language, and customs, and names, then the following generation reverts to custom, giving their grandparents' names to their children, visiting—and finding some of their identity in—the old country, so it is with families and adoption.

This is important to note. Patterns caused by loss, secrecy, and only a partial understanding of adoption are passed down in families from one generation to the next. Judith, when she'd made the decision to telephone Rose's family, had been pregnant and not married. She had decided to parent her child. There was a need to tell her birth grandmother that "I am keeping *my* baby even though you gave *yours* (my mother) away." Judith had in a sense been given too little choice in the pattern she was entering into: when there are secrets, there is no control of choice-making for those who inherit them.

Sam began to feel better, and as if he understood the situation he'd been thrust into. "How long do I have to be in this therapy?" he asked eventually. I answered, "Well, whenever you feel you're done, Sam, you're done." I explained that with my "brief-long-term" therapy arrangement, he could always come back and visit any time he felt the need.

Sam said, "But wait—there's one last thing I want to do. I want to give my wife a gift. There is something that she did not complete in her life and I want to complete it for her. I want to meet her daughter, Edith, and her granddaughter, Judith. I want to do this for Rose, but I want to meet them just once." He said, "May I do that here? I don't want them to come to my house and I don't want to meet at some restaurant or strange place." I said, "Absolutely." Edith and Judith were called, and they agreed to come. Sam asked how he should prepare and I suggested he might have some copies of some of the pictures that he'd showed me made for them. He might tell them stories about Rose and her family and he could give them some medical information. Sam knew he didn't want an awkward meeting to occur in the waiting room, so he arranged to come a half-hour early with his daughter Linda and her husband, David. We were sitting in my office when the receptionist called and said the other family had arrived.

I opened the door to my office. Standing before me was Rose! It was astounding. Edith looked exactly like the pictures I had seen of Rose. And if this was a shock for me, you can imagine how it affected Linda and Sam. Edith, her husband, her son, and Judith with her baby all walked into the office and seated themselves. The entire family had come for this session. Sam told stories about his wife and gave Edith copies of photographs of Rose he'd had made.

In the midst of the session, Edith looked over to Sam and asked, "What would you be to me, Sam?" "Well, I guess I'd sort of be your stepfather," he said. And she said, with tears in her eyes, "I would have been very proud to have had you for my father." After this wonderful exchange, Sam explained how he'd wanted this moment in time for them all. It was his gift to Rose and to them from Rose. He said he did not feel he wanted a continuing relationship, and Edith's family said they understood this.

After this very moving session, there were still unresolved issues. It had been extremely difficult for Linda to see that her half-sister looked so much like Rose—almost exactly as she had looked when Linda was a child, since Edith was that much older than Linda. It was an eerie experience for her. It often is. In the world of adoption, we call Linda's status that of "second first child."

When the birth parents marry and have subsequent children—usually not telling the world about the child they have placed—the second first child, or the one who has always been the first child to the rest of the world, is the one who is most affected by a search and reunion. When this second first child discovers that he or she is not, after all, the oldest in the family, or that he or she is not, after all, the only girl or the only boy, it displaces them in a profound and shocking way. Often this child is the sibling who has the hardest time accepting the adopted person. This was true for Linda.

Sam came back for a "50,000-mile checkup" eventually and said, "Well, I'm sleeping and eating and Linda is feeling better now too. I feel that all is at rest for Rose as well. The only one who doesn't know what's happened is my youngest son, but he lives far away with his wife and children." I said, "Sam, someone once told me that the grave spews up secrets! What will happen if you have an accident and your son discovers this news after you're gone, and he finds that others knew and he didn't? You can relate to how it might feel, can't you Sam?" Sam said, "I *knew* you would say this!" and he then agreed to tell his youngest son.

✤

Sam's story underlines the issue of secrecy versus privacy, which I think is an important distinction, especially in adoption. We've seen that secrecy too often has been a corrosive influence on birth parents' lives, as for Rose and Sam and for Claire. Too often, adoption has a great deal of secrecy surrounding it for everyone involved. For adoptive parents who have not been helped to understand that grief over infertility can be a normal part of the adoption process, secrecy concerning these feelings can prevent them from healing. For birth and adoptive children not told the truth about their or their siblings' origins, secrecy can have a profound effect on their ability to trust and to form identity. Throughout this book you'll read stories that illustrate the damaging effects of secrecy on families' lives.

And yet I feel strongly that secrecy is not usually the fault of the birth or adoptive families, but of the system and the professionals in it who do not respect these people enough to feel that they can manage their own lives and their own stories. Too often it is the system of adoption, with its sealed birth records and its legal fictions—falsified birth certificates—that creates an aura of secrecy, that attempts to erase the truth that, for the child, needs to be acknowledged, not denied.

Privacy in adoption is, I think, a different matter. People need to have boundaries. They need to use discretion in what they talk about and with whom they talk. Secrecy is when things about *you* are kept from *you*. Privacy is when *you choose* to whom you want to tell things about yourself.

As we discuss the family situation in adoption, it becomes clear that one thing that should be private is any discussion about the adoption of a particular child. Many kids who come in to see me are upset that their parents are discussing their adoption with a stranger or a neighbor in the supermarket. It is that child's *privacy* that is being violated when this happens. The family may have many discussions at home about adoption and may tell the story of the adoption of each child nightly. The problem is having many strangers know the story of the child before the child is ready to hear it in full, or when the child wants to choose not to have these particular people talk about her story.

This may happen even more frequently with transracial and international adoptions when the parents and child look so obviously different or speak different languages. It may be quite obvious that the child is adopted. But the issue of privacy is very important, and a child can feel invaded by having it discussed at a time when it doesn't feel appropriate or comfortable to him.

Birth parents never lose their role as those who gave birth to the child. The child's connection to the past is through this birth mother and father and their genes and stories. The story may be sad, or hard, or even horrible, but it is the true story for a child who is adopted. The fact of adoption means that the birth parents do not have the role of "parent." It does not mean that they do not have the role of caring, and thinking about the child, and maybe even wishing things had been different. We continue to have funny notions about what a birth parent is. If we care about the children, we must have some positive and even loving thoughts about the people who gave them life.

Chapter 2
Parental rites: The adoptive parent

Adoption is often the first choice for a couple or individual wanting children. Many single parents and gay or lesbian parents choose adoption as a way to parent. And there are heterosexual couples who always wanted to adopt as well as to have birth children, or who want and feel they can provide for a larger family through adoption.

Still, of the singles and couples we see who are trying to make the decision whether or not to adopt, most have come to this point because of infertility. Usually, one member of a couple is more prepared to move beyond medical, surgical, and pharmacological fertility procedures into the realm of adoption. It is important to work carefully with couples about their feelings concerning infertility and adoption, as individuals and as a couple, and to educate them thoroughly about the choices they might have in the adoption process. People often feel defeated and powerless as they are struggling with infertility. For instance, if the woman is the one who is dealing physically with the invasiveness of fertility treatments—the medical interventions, the shots, the surgical procedures—she may be more ready to put the physical/emotional trauma of infertility treatment behind her and start her family by adoption. The planned sex and the weight of worrying about how, when, or whether pregnancy will occur, affect the couple relationship—sometimes for the better and sometimes for the worse. Many couple and family therapists are not well enough aware of how delicate the couple relationship is at this time, and how emotions concerning infertility and the idea of adoption are related.

When the decision is made to consider adopting a baby, it is not always *totally* made. It may sound harsh, but adoption is the second choice. In the best of all worlds, the birth parents would not be dealing with an untimely pregnancy and the painful decision not to parent their child. In the best of all worlds, the couple struggling with infertility and planning to adopt would have been able to give birth to a child.

By the time adoption is the choice, most couples are ready for that decision. Adoption may have been the second choice, yet the child is most certainly not. The bottom line is that these folks want to parent. (And the bottom line with many birth parents is that they can't parent at this particular time and that infants and children can't be put on hold indefinitely.)

It is important to acknowledge—here's another place in this discussion when truth is important—that in the back of the adopting parents' minds there is still the hope that they will eventually become pregnant. There are many examples of people who do get pregnant right after an adoption, and so many prospective adoptive parents are holding this as a hope. Of course, we know that adoption does not make pregnancy happen, but we also see that a pregnancy may follow an adoption. For the vast majority of adoptive parents, though, as we have learned from our clients in their fifties, sixties, and seventies, adoption doesn't, and never will, fix infertility.

The issues of infertility stay with people throughout their lives, even when they parent children through adoption. This is a fact that we have not paid attention to until quite recently. It is important for people considering adoption to know this, so that they are not led to believe that they will be cured of their loss and then feel disappointed by the feelings of loss that continue to ebb and flow throughout their lifetime.

Parents preparing to adopt are often so busy with all that must be done psychologically and emotionally as well as bureaucratically that they forget to begin educating their extended family. Without passing on reading materials, and having some conversations about how to talk about adoption, the adoptive individual or couple may be shocked at the things relatives say.

❖

Betsy was an adult adopted person and a client who began in one session to think about times in her life when she had been most aware of being adopted. She started to describe to me her eighth birthday. For this special birthday, she and her mother had decided their project was to make Betsy's room a big-girl's room. They chose wallpaper, and paint, and fabric for curtains and they did the whole room by themselves. It was great fun and they were both excited and pleased with the results. The grandparents were there for Betsy's birthday dinner. After the cake, Betsy and her mother each took one of Nana's hands and told her to close her eyes and they would lead her to a surprise. They walked her down the hallway to the bedroom door and told her to open her eyes. She did. She looked around the room and finally said, "What a beautiful room for someone else's child."

I wonder, for the grandmother to have said something so terribly unkind, how much unacknowledged sadness and disappointment she felt herself over her son and daughter-in-law's infertility and the fact that Betsy was not her own genetic grandchild. We don't often realize that grandparents are at the stage of generativity. They are aware that their lives will be over soon and they want to have left something and someone behind.

Educating the extended family about adoption issues and feelings that may recur is essential to the well-being of the adoptive family, and should be included, ideally, as part of the preadoptive process for all families.

❖

It is during the preadoptive stage that parents-to-be are most vulnerable and inexperienced and that agencies and adoption professionals too often work against the child's welfare—and so against the adoptive families' interests as well.

In working with couples and individuals who are thinking of adoption, it is essential to do a great deal of "psychoeducation." They must be given historical, developmental, and longitudinal information about adoptive parenting. Some of the issues that will come up for them must be explained to prepare them for the challenges ahead. We must work closely with these prospective parents to help them to understand what kinds of choices they have. These choices will affect their lives and beyond.

Do they want to adopt domestically or internationally?
Do they want to adopt a child of the same race?

Do they want an infant or an older child?
Do they want to adopt from a public child welfare agency or
    from a private agency or attorney?

There are so many choices these days among agencies and private and independent sources, depending on the state. Often preadoptive people do not know what each of these adoptions means and entails. It would be most helpful for prospective parents to have a chance to understand the implications and lifelong effects of each of these choices.

Many people felt and feel safer with international adoptions, for instance, because, in their fear of birth parents, they believe that this will avoid any conflict or need to search. We have learned over the years that this is far from the truth.

Adopters need to be informed, first, to make a choice that is truly going to feel right for *their* family, and, second, to be clear enough so that the agency or professional working with them will know which child will benefit most in the long term from becoming a member of their family. Again, and I can't say this enough, *adoption is about finding families for children, not about finding children for families.*

In recent years, since the availability of white infants for domestic adoptions has declined because of social acceptance of single parenting, birth control, and abortion, and increasing support for family preservation, many couples seeking to adopt have had to partake of whatever "program" is being offered, whether through a certain country or by a particular agency or professional.

By the time most people get to the decision of adoption, they are tired of all that they have been through and simply want to start their family. They want the shortest line to the baby in their arms or the child in their home and heart. This is easy to understand, but it is not in the best interest of the child or of the parents. The shortest line is not always the right line for a particular family.

Once one is in line with an adoption agency or lawyer, only the particular kind of adoption that they do is offered and the prospective parent has little or no say. There is little consideration of what kind of family you are or what kind of child would be best in your family. Home studies for parents hoping to adopt feel like one more hoop to jump through, and, in fact, the way that most of them are done they are little more than that. Applicants are almost unanimously approved. They are observed and asked to write some things and have a few visits with and from a social worker and then approximately ninety-eight percent are approved.

Why wouldn't they make good parents? They want to be parents. They are going out of their way to say that that is what they want. They have been through a lot, and are consciously and conscientiously making this decision. But they are approved in general. No thought is given to the adults' attachment styles. No attention is given to experiences they've had which might lend themselves to working with a particular kind of child, with a particular temperament or background.

Before adopting, most parents are not given the education that they need to decide what kind of adoption will be best for them, but, more important, best for a child. The *home study* of the 1940s should now be a *family study* to look for the best environment for a particular child.

The Center For Family Connections works in a very different way with these couples and individuals than an adoption agency or adoption attorney does, because we have a different orientation. One of the things that we do is to have them focus on what they are doing and to make decisions that take into consideration their entire life cycle— not just this moment in time.

When approaching an agency or adoption professional who will be making the decision about placing a child in one's care, there is a tendency to try to conform and to look as nearly perfect as possible. For a heterosexual couple, this often means that one person suppresses any fears and hesitations rather than bringing them out in the open. For gay and lesbian couples, it is common for one partner to adopt as a single person, which means that the other partner doesn't get the necessary education and counseling about the enormity of co-parenting a child. We end up hurting families by indirectly encouraging them to lie.

A China story

Preadoptive parents are often in a very vulnerable position. This story sounds unique, but unfortunately, I have heard it about eight times now on both the East and West coasts. The preadoptive parent finally gets the call and goes off on the very long journey to China to claim her child.

When she arrives, an extremely sick infant is shown to her. The agency personnel, the Chinese officials—everyone—tell her that the baby is too critically ill and that she will not live. The mother has already attached to this sickly baby and has been thinking about her on the long flight. She is jet-lagged, overwhelmed, and everyone says that she cannot take this sick baby back home.

Before going to China, all of the paperwork was done on the baby that was to be hers. Now she is given a new baby. A well baby. This baby has a name and history, too. But the bureaucracy requires that the sickly baby's paperwork be applied to the new baby so that this mother can leave with her group and return to the United States. The mother knows that she has false papers on this baby. Months later, she meets me at a conference in San Francisco after a lecture and asks if she can speak with me. She tells me the story. One that I have heard before. She is concerned because she knows that someday her child will want to know about her past. If her daughter looks at these papers, they will be false. They will be wrong.

What is this mother to do? I told her that she now had some insight into the experience of a birth mother. She has had to leave behind a child that she could not parent. She can use this experience as a way to empathize and understand the terribly sad position of the Chinese birth mother, and she can use this feeling and experience to relate to her own daughter. She must always tell the truth, but tell it in ways that make sense to the child developmentally.

Adoption is very simple if you think of the child only as a baby. Most people can love a baby easily and almost immediately. Yet if parents don't confront their own more complicated beliefs and fantasies about their life as a family with their adopted child, they invariably face problems later on within their own family as the child grows, and as the family has to interact with the larger society.

We encourage people to confront these issues in an open and honest way in the course of their consultations with us, so that they can make an informed and lifelong decision that will be not only in their best interest but, most especially, in the child's. In the four sections that follow, on international adoption, interracial adoption, sick baby adoption, and older child adoption, I tell stories about these especially challenging forms of adoption. Without the possibility of thinking about all of these examples, it is hard for a family to truly take the adoption process into their own hands and decide what kind of family they are and what child they would best serve as a family.

International adoption

Most people setting out to adopt spend a relatively short time reading and learning about adoptions and then go to an agency or adoption professional. If infertility is their reason for pursuing adoption, they are, as I've said, exhausted and frustrated by the medical and surgical interventions, the disappointments, and the wait. They simply want a baby; they want the shortest line.

The agency's or adoption professional's connection to a country and the country's economy and political situation all affect what kinds of adoptions are quickest then and there.

A few years ago, when the short line was for Romanian babies, a couple came in to see me. They said they were fighting about adoption. The wife, Lori, had been down the fertility procedures route and was fed up. She simply wanted a baby. Now. The husband, George, was still grieving that they weren't able to have a birth child. One day, in my office, after they knew they were soon to be matched with a Romanian child, George said, "Hey, honey, we better hide the silverware. Those little gypsy kids will steal anything!" I asked what Lori thought of that statement. She said that George just had an odd sense of humor. I suggested that what he said may have been meant as a joke, but if it suggested what he was feeling about the Romanian child, it would be a serious problem in their family. I recommended that they do one of two things: either forget about Romania and investigate adoption from a different country or a domestic adoption; or learn more about Romania so that they would not hold a racist and skewed view of the children of that country. The couple chose the latter course, and they now, ten years later, have a twelve-year-old Romanian daughter who is thriving and whose parents are culturally sensitive to her country and to her culture of origin.

Often, the countries that we adopt from—the sending countries—are those that are in the news because of terrible problems, such as war, the collapse of a regime, poverty. The adoptive parents have to be aware that their attitude toward the country of origin will eventually affect their child's sense of identity and self-esteem. A child, and eventually the adult the child becomes, will search in many ways for his birth mother and father, but also for mother country and fatherland. The couple or individual thinking of adopting must examine what their feelings are about that country truthfully. They must find ways to provide the child with cultural information that will build a positive identity. As in cases where there are complex and painful truths about birth parents, it is quite possible to find some good—in family history and in cultural/political history—that can be conveyed to the child. Just as birth and adoptive parents must have a positive regard for each other, the adoptive child's parents must work to understand and communicate the positive, special aspects of their child's country of origin.

Transracial adoption

For the transracial adoptive families we work with, we recommend that the adoptive parents see themselves as a transracial family, rather than seeing the child as a child of another race. It is essential that they live in areas where there are friends and professionals of the same ethnic and racial background in the community, people who will be natural role models for the child. Children need to have these kinds of connections. A family that cannot understand that a transracially placed child will need connection to, and understanding about, his or her culture and race in order to be prepared to be in the world as an adolescent and adult may not be the family that can raise that particular child.

Parents who are not, themselves, sensitive to institutional racism may sometimes not notice that their child—the only child of color in her grade or perhaps entire school—is having to handle a great deal as a very young child. One of my clinicians on the PACT team, I remember, was very upset by an incident that resulted in a major change for a family he was counseling. The family had adopted a very dark-skinned African American child and lived in a very white suburb. The child, who was outgoing and wonderful, was excited because his class was doing a play and he wanted to act and to sing in it. One day he came home crying and his parents asked what was wrong. He said that he could not be in the play because he did not have "a sunshiny face." The family did not take this as a racial comment initially, until their therapy session when the clinician asked if they felt any of the anger that he was feeling as he heard this. They were at first shocked and then very angry. The family confronted the teacher and the school about this problem and, when they felt they were not being heard, made slow and careful arrangements to move to a more integrated area so that their child, and they, would not be so alone. Throughout this book there are many stories about the issues that transracially adopted children and adults confront in their lives.

Transracial adoptions are increasing. We must guarantee that the families adopting these children are well aware of what the long-range needs of the children are. The preadoptive parents must be able to put their own egos aside and pay attention to the needs of these children— which is, after all, an integral ingredient of parenting.

Special-needs infant and toddler adoptions

I once saw a family that had come in for family therapy about six months after a baby had been placed with them but before the adoption was finalized. They had just learned that their baby was HIV positive. They also had a four-year-old adopted child in the family and needed to make a decision as a family whether to return the six-month-old baby to the agency. They questioned whether they could parent a child with HIV.

They were, of course, frightened, worried, ashamed, angry, and grieving. In the course of the family therapy, we talked about the no-win situation they were in.

How would the four-year-old feel if they returned a baby who was "sick"? What would that mean to her? What would happen when she got sick? How would they handle the impact this would have on her? What about the four-year-old's belief that adoption was forever? How would they deal with the fact that she had already begun to have a real relationship with her baby brother? How would they feel about her loss? How would they feel about the loss of the child through death? The couple had already lost a child at birth before they'd decided to adopt. These were stressful family therapy sessions regarding a painful decision.

In the long run, the family decided to parent this child. They come in occasionally for a checkup, and everything is going well. They are relieved that they made the decision they did, and there are, as yet, no huge medical problems. They are very attached to the child.

The adoptive parents are aware that there will be challenges and problems down the road. They are dealing not only with questions and concerns about adoption, but also with those about HIV and AIDS.

Many of the families that we see now have adopted babies that were born with fetal alcohol syndrome, with positive toxic screens for crack or heroin, or with AIDS. These adoptive parents come in for services sooner and need a great deal of support as well as an array of post-adoptive services of a different kind than parents with physically healthy infants. This is true whether the parents intentionally adopted a child who was ill or the child's condition was not clear at the time of adoption. Either way, parents are seeing differences in these children and wanting to know how best to serve them as a family.

Daisy's story   Daisy was born with a positive toxic screen for drugs at birth and was placed immediately in a foster home. The same foster family loved her and cared for her for her first two and a half years. In that Latino family there was an eight-year-old birth child who played with and took care of Daisy and loved her very much. The pediatrician did a test on Daisy for HIV after learning that the birth mother had AIDS. The day that the results came back, the social worker called Mrs. Ramirez and told her that Daisy was HIV positive. Mrs. Ramirez panicked. She was fearful for the lives of her other children. She called her husband at his job and told him. He said Daisy must go. Now. Mrs. Ramirez dropped Daisy off with a green garbage bag filled with her toys and clothes at the Department of Social Services office nearby. Daisy was placed in a preadoptive home. The parents were a lesbian couple who were very understanding of her needs and not fearful of her illness. One member of the couple was a nurse who works with HIV patients. Daisy was also placed in a special daycare center for kids who are HIV positive. Caroline and Anne, Daisy's new parents, wanted her to have some kind of connection to her foster family. We arranged for a consultation. The Ramirez family were eager to come. Mrs. Ramirez now wished she had not acted so hastily. Her eight-year-old was grieving terribly and was very angry at the parents for "throwing" Daisy away. During the consultation, Lydia brought some toys for Daisy, one of which was a harmonica. Lydia played it and then gave it to Daisy who happily played it and then handed it back to Lydia. Mrs. Ramirez leapt across the floor and grabbed it in midair before it touched Lydia's lips. This was a clear demonstration of her lack of education about AIDS and her lack of sensitivity to Daisy. We explained to Mrs. Ramirez that Daisy could not be bounced back and forth and that she was now in a permanent home that was sensitive to her needs. The family wished to maintain some relationship and to allow Lydia and Daisy to be "cousins." Mr. Ramirez was angry that his daughter Lydia was so sad and that a lesbian couple had Daisy. Mrs. Ramirez just cried. Caroline and Anne were empathetic and offered to educate them about the disease and about how to be cautious, knowing that they feared that Lydia or their other children would contract the disease from Daisy. The families have become friends and extended family, and Daisy has the very strong love and connection that she needs as a little girl with many challenges to face in her possibly shortened life.

Older child adoption

With older child placements and in situations when the birth parents—especially the birth mother—have serious problems, it is important to find a way to maintain a connection if the plan for that child to stay loyal and permanently connected to the family that is raising him or her is to be successful.

Shanea's story   Shanea had a very hard life and knew nothing else. Not only had she spent most of her years in the public system but so had her mother and grandmother before her. Shanea had addictions. Shanea had been abused repeatedly since the age of eight and had used drugs and alcohol since age twelve. Shanea had five children living in foster care: her oldest daughter Linnea, who was fourteen; two sons, Lincoln, age ten, and Lavance, age eight; her daughter Laquanda, age six, and the youngest daughter, Lyndell, age four. Linnea had been the "parentified" child who had taken care of her mother when she was on drugs as well as taking care of her siblings. Shanea rarely took care of the children; she would leave them with relatives and friends or sometimes just leave them by themselves. They had been removed by the Department of Social Services and placed in foster homes early on. When Shanea would try to recover from her addictions they would be returned to her and then found to be abused and neglected again and taken back into the system. There was one social worker who had known the extended family and these kids for years and became the most consistent person in their lives. Her name was Ellery Davis, and she tried her hardest to keep the children together in one foster home. This was not always possible. At one point, all five were in a home together. Throughout this time, they had supervised visits at the agency office with their mother when she was sober. Ellery supervised the visits and knew how important they were, to the older kids especially. If time went by and Linnea did not have a visit with her mom, she would begin to panic. She felt responsible for the health and safety of her mom and siblings. She was only fourteen and yet the weight of the world had always been on her. Laquanda, age six, died while the children were in one foster home. It was an accident, but with suspicious undertones. All children were removed from this particular foster home and placed, in emergency, in many different situations. Ellery knew that the death of a sister in this close sibling group was loss enough; they needed to be together. She worked day and night to find a home that would take all four of the remaining sibs. She also wanted a permanent plan for them, not more shuffling in the foster care system. The Center For Family Connections was called in as consultant on this case. It was clear to us that these children would not deal with adoption well unless it was an open arrangement that allowed continued supervised visits with Mom.

Ellery found a seasoned couple who had birth children, adopted children, and foster children. Many of their kids were grown up and had left home. They lived in a neighborhood that included extended family, close friends, and church community. They had resources and support. They came forward and wanted to take the remaining four kids permanently and to keep them together. Mr. Leroy Willis was a superb father and foster father. He had had a personal experience of early loss and splitting in his family of origin and had a huge commitment to keeping siblings together. He and his wife, Edna, had spent a lifetime making family for themselves by making family for children who needed it. They had no trepidations about the continued connection to the birth mother. This seemed like an ideal situation.

Remember that these are four children who, even before the

death of their sister, had suffered extreme neglect, abuse, and loss and now were grieving and suffering once again. These are all special needs kids, each with his or her own very special needs. It would be a huge feat to parent one of these children, but to take on all four was a mountainous task. The Willis family was up for it. We met with the Willises and we found them to be knowledgeable about what they were going to encounter and ready to rise to the occasion.

We also met with Shanea. Shanea was frightened. She was in a treatment program and was doing well. Finally, after four years, her name came up for a large enough subsidized apartment to care for her kids. She knew, however, that if she tried too soon, she would end up back on drugs. She was clear that although she was beginning to seem "fit to parent," she was really just getting used to living without her drugs and alcohol and that this was a tenuous time. We talked about the fact that she was and would always be the mother of these children, but that she had, in fact, never been their parent. We asked if she would meet with the Willis family. Shanea was scared. Twice before her children had been ready for adoption and she had been called in to the Department of Social Services to have a "termination" visit with them. When the first placement fell apart before finalization, a second "termination" visit was arranged. What this taught the kids was that adoption would mean never knowing if their mom was okay and so they sabotaged each placement.

How could we do this differently? How could we allow the kids to keep having contact with Mom, but to have the security and healing time of a permanent family?

The day that the Willises met Shanea was a moving one. Shanea was a nervous wreck. She had to call her alcohol counselor eight times from our office. When the Willises came in, Edna handed two gifts to Shanea, who looked shocked. "Who are these for?" "What is this?" she asked. "They are gifts for you, Shanea," said Edna. "You are giving us the greatest gift of all by letting us parent your children. We want to give you something as well." Shanea had a tear in her eye as she opened the presents. One was a beautiful frame with a spiritual poem in it, and the other was a more beautiful frame with a lovely picture of all five of the children. Ellery had shown it to Edna and they had decided to have copies made so that everyone could have one.

The Willises told Shanea that they would want her to be a part of the lives of the children, but that they, as the parents, would have to decide when that would happen and what was best. They suggested that Ellery act as an intermediary for letters and pictures and that they use Ellery's office before finalization and the Center afterward for clinically supervised visits with the kids and Shanea. We talked about how Linnea might need more frequent visits than the younger kids. Shanea said that this seemed like the right thing to do.

We had several sessions with the kids, alone and together. We worked with all components of this soon-to-be-family. And at the last meeting prior to the placement of the kids with the Willises we had a ceremony in our office. We had the new parents and Shanea and all four children along with pictures of Laquanda. We have Polaroid cameras ever-ready for photos at these precious meetings so that people can have pictures to hold onto.

The ceremony consisted of Shanea placing the hands of her four children and the picture of the fifth child in the hands of Leroy and Edna and telling them that she gave them permission to be the parents of her children. She told the children, as did Leroy and Edna, that she would always be their mother, but that she had not been their parent and that they really needed to have parents as well as a mom. She wanted them to have the stability that neither she nor her mother had had growing up. She wanted them to make her proud and she wanted to keep in touch in the ways that she had been doing for the past fourteen years. Shanea told them that she was recovering and that she hoped that she would be available to them in more ways in the coming years, but that she could not count on it and so they could not either. It was moving to witness.

Bonding and transitions

Many parents do not understand that *all* parents taking their child home—whether it is the first, second, or third child, or whether the child is adopted or born into the family—have to *develop a relationship* with that child, that person. This is where and when attachment begins.

Attachment is the relationship that both birth mother and birth father, or adoptive parents, or foster parents have to *develop* with the child, and the child also has to develop this new relationship with the parents.

Sometimes parents have a hard time if a child is not quick to attach. Some parents feel rejected by the child and this starts the relationship off in an awkward way. Even with birth parents and child, attachment is not always automatic. Some relationships take more work than others, and it is the job of the adult—the parent—to work on this attachment process.

Many children who are adopted, both domestically and internationally, are still in shock from the trauma of leaving the familiar person, their birth mother, or from the cumulative trauma of moves from foster home to orphanage. Sometimes this is compounded by physical or sexual abuse or neglect. We know, from the perinatal psychologists, that infants clearly identify who their birth parents are by smells and sounds and that they do have grave reactions to loss.

Some people find ways to attach instantly and simply do it. Other people need some help if they are having difficulty making the attachment to a child or if the child is having trouble attaching to the family.

Some parents are embarrassed by this lack of automatic connection. They may feel rejected or ashamed and, often, they do not seek the help that they very much need. This is the time that attachment can be *best* treated. This is the time when the connections can be made in ways that will be everlasting.

These crises are not the crises that everyone experiences, but when families are having difficulties in the first few days of having the baby, or child, at home, it would help if they thought of this as a normal situation for any child who is in shock.

As in all cases of shock, the child may be overly adaptive for a length of time, and these issues may only surface later, seemingly out of the blue. It may be a case of a child now feeling safe enough to move from shock to his true feelings, and for some parents, this will feel like a rejection. It will help families to have some understanding that these feelings and reactions are *very* normal and that they can be worked with from the start to create an environment of attachment that will last.

With an older child and some internationally placed older children there is often a need for postadoptive services earlier on during the transition and settling-in time. The work done at this time can often prevent later problems for the family and the child, and can give the child an opportunity to begin to make sense of the complexity of adoption.

Transitions are so very important for infants and children. We often neglect to take the time to make the transition smooth and careful. We would do a great deal toward building attachment if we paid better attention to transitions.

It is normal, for instance, for a new parent, upon receiving her infant baby in China, to want to take all of the worn and dirty clothing from the orphanage off and to wash the baby clean and put on the new American clothing—maybe baby GAP—that has been specially bought. This is, however, taking away the comfort, the familiar feel and smell that would make a transition smoother and would help in the process of attaching. There are things that seem to meet the instinctual needs of the parents—to claim the child, to make the child their own. Often these are the very things that are not in the best interest of a smooth and gradual transition for the child.

Joby's story   Attachment requires the emotional adoption of a child, not just the legal adoption. My Center contracts with the state to do consultations on difficult adoption cases and other permanency plans for children in care. We had a call a few years ago about a family who had adopted two siblings through the Department of Social Services. The adoptions were both finalized. The family was calling because they wanted to return one of the children they had adopted to the state. The adoption was disrupting and potentially dissolving. Linda and Ernst Shultz were a great couple and had been wonderful parents to their only child, Ernst, Jr. E.J. was six years old and had been the perfect child, and they the perfect parents. They had wanted a larger family, but had secondary infertility and could not produce another child.

They grieved, they thought, they researched, and they then decided to adopt. They wanted to adopt a toddler so they went to the public agency, the Department of Social Services. They were trained, along with other potential adoptive parents in a ten-week course. They were eager to enlarge their family.

The social worker called one day and said that she had a great two-and-a-half-year-old child available for adoption. His name was Davin and he was a great kid. Already, on the phone, Linda had begun the emotional adoption of Davin. Sentences later, the social worker mentioned that Davin had an older brother, Joby, and that the two could not be placed separately. Joby was six years old. The Shultzes discussed this dilemma between themselves. They felt torn. They only wanted one child—a toddler. But then, why would they not take the sibling of this child that they had already emotionally become attached to. So they agreed.

Joby and E.J. suddenly became "twins" who were far from twins. Both were aged six and that is where the similarity ended. E.J. had had everything he had ever wanted and had never experienced a loss. He was a great kid and shared well with his new brother at first, but it was hard. Joby had been moved six times in his six years. Many times, all of his possessions had been left behind. He had cared for his mother when she was sick on drugs and he had cared, all of the time, for his baby brother Davin. He was a parentified child who it seemed could not be parented. He did not trust adults. Why should he? It was hard to get him to let Linda and Ernst parent Davin.

Joby was a difficult and challenging kid, just what you would expect after his many traumatic life experiences of the past six years. Linda and Ernst could not handle him. A year after the legalization, they wanted it to end. DSS sent them to our Center for a consultation. They arrived with a social worker who had been assigned to them (a new one).

Family sculpture is a very revealing family therapy technique. As the "sculptor," one member of the family fashions the family into a live sculpture, placing the others where he feels they are in relation to each other and to the sculptor. I asked Joby to do a family sculpture for me, and I explained to them all what it was. Joby set his family up in sculpture form as he saw them. He put his Linda and Ernst on the couch and little Davin on Linda's lap. He put Ernst's arm around E.J.'s shoulder, and then he ran around the room.

I asked him to put himself in the sculpture as well. He said, as he ran around and around the room, "I am in the sculpture. I'm an airplane with no place to land."

That one moving picture was worth a thousand words.

You see, Linda and Ernst legally adopted both of the children, but they only emotionally adopted Davin. In order for the family to truly work, they would have to emotionally adopt Joby as well. There are many children who are adopted legally but not emotionally by one or, as in Joby's case, both of their parents. Sometimes only one partner in a couple really wants to adopt and truly emotionally adopts, although both become the legal parents. In order for families to be strong and capable of handling the challenges that adoption presents, they must adopt the children fully and wholly, legally and emotionally. Attachment is not something that happens only on the part of the children. The parents must attach as well.

The au pair

Today, we have many parents who must both work to support themselves and, often in private adoptions, to afford the expense of the adoption. For attachment to take place, it is strongly recommended that the adoptive parents take a period of time to have the child become comfortable and safe in the new environment and to understand who the new parents are. A succession of full-time babysitters can cause an adopted child to feel the trauma of abandonment over and over. The child has bonded physiologically to a birth mother and has been moved and placed at least once, if not more times, with foster parents and orphanages. The adopted child and adoptive parents must go through the attachment process.

Parents certainly could use and deserve some advice before the adoption about how best to transition the new baby or child into the family and how to facilitate an attachment that will be strong and secure. The parents' attachment style has a strong effect on how quickly the child will adapt and the child's ability to adapt in a healthy way. We also include babysitters and au pairs in the family therapy. We feel that these employees are the daytime and after-school caregivers, and often the children will talk about adoption with them. It is best for the caregivers to be educated by the adoptive parents about how they wish to have the subject of adoption handled with the children. Just as I mentioned earlier, the grandparents, extended family, and others who are close to the family need to have a good understanding of the underpinnings of adoption in order to answer the child's questions and in order to be sure to convey positive messages about adoption to the child.

The job of any parent is a huge one. The job of parenting an adopted child is filled with additional challenges, and the more we equip the parents and their support network, the better able to meet the challenges they will be. Preadoptive parent education and empowerment in all of these issues are what will change the system to one that is about the best interests of the child.

It is with that in mind that I wrote this poem to adoptive parents:

You cannot change the truth.
These are your children,
but they came from somewhere else.
And they are the children of those places
and of those people as well.

Help them to know about their past
and about their present.
Help them to know that they are from extended families,
that they have only one parent or set of parents,
but that they have more mothers and fathers.
They have grandmothers, godmothers, birth mothers, mother countries,
mother earth.
They have grandfathers, godfathers, birth fathers, and fatherlands.
They have family by birth and by adoption.
They have family by choice and by chance.

Childhood is short;
They are our children to raise;
they are our children to love;
and then they are citizens of the world.
What we do to them creates the world that we live in.
Give them life.
Give them their truth.
Give them love.
Give them all that they came with,
Give them all that they grow with.

Your children do not belong to you,
but they belong with you.
You cannot keep them from what is theirs, but you can keep loving them.
You do not own your children,
but they are your own.

Chapter 3
The adopted child, birth to eight years

We see many couples and individuals who come in around the time their adopted child is past toddlerhood, parents who know that they will need to tell their child about adoption soon. They want to begin to talk about adoption and to work through, as a couple or as a single parent, how they will tell the child. They want to sort out their own feelings and insecurities before they talk with their child. They know it is going to be hard to talk about adoption. Adoption brings along with it the concept of loss—the loss associated with infertility, the loss for the child of easy identity with the birth family, the loss of what might have been—and there is, inevitably some sadness attached to it.

Parents at this stage often want "just a book" or "just a pamphlet" to tell them "how to" tell their child. I always tell them I sincerely hope they won't rely on a book or pamphlet. All parents, but this is especially important with adoptive parents, at this moment need to know that *they* are the ones in charge. We may be the experts on adoption, but they are the experts on their child.

We want parents to arrive at their own natural way to tell their child about adoption—not the way some expert, or book, says it should be done. We work closely with the parent or parents to figure out what their language is, and to think about how they might begin to share the fact of adoption in a way that a child can take it in over time, at different developmental stages. Early on, the important focus is simply to make the word "adoption" familiar. Two-, three-, and four-year-olds, no matter how precocious and brilliant according to their parents, can only take in so much. Simple and truthful for the very young child is my motto.

I live in Cambridge, Massachusetts, with Harvard and M.I.T. nearby. Often in the grocery store I'll see some graduate student with his three-year-old daughter in the shopping cart. The child will ask a question, and the father will respond with a lengthy dissertation-like answer to this small child. The child actually looks like she gets it. She'll respond appropriately. You know that this father thinks his child is absolutely brilliant (and she probably is), but she is also only three years old. If you were to ask the child what she had really understood of her father's explanation, it would become clear that she'd simply liked the interaction and had responded appropriately and even taken in pieces—but not the intricacies—of the explanation. At age three, it is not possible, cognitively, to grasp a complex, abstract issue, as adoption certainly is.

What is most important at this stage is that the child hear the word *adoption* from the person she trusts and loves the most—her parent. A child should not hear it for the first time from someone in the neighborhood or from someone in the extended family who says, "Oh, you're adopted," in a way that feels shaming. The telling needs to be in words and in a way that feels positive. The word *adoption* needs to be made familiar.

After admitting that I don't think parents can rely on books for this—and there are in fact few helpful books on adoption for younger children—I do recommend *Gordon and Susan Adopt a Baby*. The story is largely about sibling rivalry between Big Bird and the new child; the word *adoption* is mentioned, really only in passing, in a simple way. It's this quite basic introduction of the word that makes the book useful for parents who are trying to find ways to make the word familiar or to begin talking about adoption.

In their nervousness, many adoptive parents try to explain the *whole* story of adoption in one sitting. It's important instead to ask the child what he or she wants to know and to respond concretely to what is being asked at that time. It often helps to ask children to explain back to you what they've been told. There is no one way we can prepare parents for how a particular child will respond. Different children make sense of this information in different ways. Some children say, "oh," and go on for a while thinking or talking very little about adoption. Some children want to know everything. In these cases, children need to be responded to as truthfully as possible, but at a developmental level that allows them to make sense of their complex situation.

I often work with couples or a single adoptive parent to help them figure out their own way of "telling." We might do role playing; we might simply have conversations about adoption so they feel comfortable talking about adoption out loud. At some point, after the parents feel they've made the word *adoption* familiar at home, they decide they want to talk about it further in my office with the child.

It's happened more than once that a child has come bounding into my office, pigtails bopping, and said, "Guess what, Joyce. I'm a doctor!" So much for careful preparation. The parents didn't realize until that very moment in my office that *adoption* had transmuted into *doctor* in the child's concrete-thinking-stage mind!

The adoptive parent role is especially challenging because they have to introduce very complex truths to a child and then be prepared to support him—even to try to stay a step ahead—as he makes sense of the truths of his life.

People—both parents and professionals—often make the mistake of thinking that adopted children don't have any concerns about adoption if they say that they don't, or if they don't ask questions. We must remember that these children are concrete thinkers and that, assuming they are with loving and good families, they, in fact, *don't* have a problem with adoption. But the question is all wrong. These children may not worry about *adoption,* but rather what came before it. Why was I not kept? Where are my birth parents? Do they think of me? Will they take me back? This question can occur as either a fear or a wish, depending on whether the child is mad at his parents!

Finally, it's important to stress that "telling" doesn't just happen once, or usually in the same way twice. Parents need to understand this and to work to feel comfortable, themselves, dealing with their own confused feelings about the birth parents, or birth family, or foster family, or birth race. These are not easy issues and they tend to pop up without warning.

Both partners need to be prepared to talk about these things and need to have a common understanding about how they will do this. These are conversations that are best planned well before they come up on the spur of the moment, as the following story illustrates.

Doug and Nancy's story   Doug and Nancy, who had a four-, almost five-year-old son named Adam, came in to talk about adoption. Doug told me that Nancy was the one who dealt with emotion in the family and that she would be doing all the talking about adoption. I warned him that Adam might want to talk to his father rather than his mother about these things at some time. Nancy and I made him role play talking to Adam about adoption. He hated to but eventually went along.

A year later they came in for a "50,000-mile checkup." (This is what we call a return visit in my "brief-long-term therapy" model.) Doug said, "Boy, was I glad you guys made me do those stupid role plays! We were skiing in Vermont and I was suspended above a mountain in a chair lift with Adam when he asked me to tell him about his birth mom! If you hadn't made me practice, I might have had to jump!"

Children are as protective of their parents as parents are of their children. It's possible that Adam once asked his mother if he grew in her tummy. If he were to see her sadness or feel it, he might, at that moment, decide that he would never again ask her anything like that. Adam might have realized that he would feel more comfortable talking to the parent who is actually less emotional—the result being, ironically, that his father, the one who likes least to talk about emotions, is asked the hardest questions.

❖

When a child begins to ask about birth parents, there is one essential need that all adoptive parents can meet, no matter how little information they may have about the birth parents. Children at this age need to know that they are human, that they were made just like any other human and had a normal gestation and birth. The only thing that sets them apart is that, after their birth, they were placed in a new family. Very often we give adopted children a story about their adoption, but no story about their beginning—about how they began in the world or where they came from. This is why many adopted people can relate so well to Superman, dropped from Krypton and found in a field by the nice Kent couple, who adopted him and called him Clark. Superman leads two lives, the one as Clark Kent and the other that reveals his identity as a member of his birth galaxy—and birth family.

In the chapter on pre- and early adolescence and on adolescence and early adulthood, I'll say more about the adopted person's need for connection to his origins that a birth story gives. The essential thing for the younger child to know is that she was born out of a seed and egg and had a birth mother and birth father like everyone else, whether she is adopted into a single-parent family, whether she is a product of donor insemination, or whether she is in a two-parent adoptive family.

School issues

Without an understanding of the challenges the adopted child, birth family, and adoptive family can face, schools and other community institutions often, unwittingly, work against the best interest of adoptees and adoptive families.

If there is very little adoption education and training for our child psychiatrists, pediatricians, psychologists, social workers, and marriage and family therapists, then there is even less for our teachers, guidance counselors, school administrators, clergy, and others who deal with the adoptee and adoptive family on a daily basis. Schools of education have done a great deal in the past decade to train teachers to be sensitive to various kinds of families in general and to create curriculum that is diverse and multicultural. These are great strides, but there are still areas of importance that are *not* touched upon. Adoption is one of them. As a result, myths and stereotypes, as well as assumptions, often take hold and underlie the thinking about and response to any behavior problems or learning problems that adopted children have in school.

For children in adoptive families, foster families, and families created through guardianship and kinship, to name a few, there is very little attention to the complex emotional issues brought up by simple and creative assignments in the schools.

I was in Berkeley, California, for instance, a couple of years ago doing some training for Bay Area therapists. I went with a friend to pick up her three-year-old at daycare. I wandered around and saw that the children's assignment had been to bring in their baby pictures (to show how much bigger they were now than those tiny babies).

But, what if a child had been in several foster homes and had no baby pictures? What if a child had come from another country at age two and had no pictures?

Many of the foster and adopted kids in these groups, I knew, would have no newborn pictures. If a child who did not have a picture acted out on this particular day, wouldn't that be an understandable way of showing his sadness and anger at not having the continuity that other children have? And yet, that acting out might be read by a teacher and by other parents as bad behavior, and that incident might mark the beginning of tracking this child as having "behavior problems."

The child in the daycare center who acts out on the day he feels conspicuously different because there is no history of his beginnings— no pictures, no stories—is not a behavior problem. That child is acting appropriately under the circumstances. Schools must be more sensitive to the complexity of the lives of adopted, foster, and guardian family children when giving assignments.

I did some consulting a few years ago for a Boston-area school for children with learning disabilities and the emotional issues that often result from them. There were 120 students in the school, 68 of whom were adopted. *More than half* the school population was adopted. The usual statistics are that in any population of learning disabled kids, about 28 percent will be adopted, which is, in itself, still quite high. Over the years both professionals and parents have had some theories about these statistics. Some say adopted children are more likely to have neurological damage. Some say the birth parents must have had attention deficit disorder, the proof being that they obviously had poor impulse control since they got themselves pregnant. Some say that the parents must have done drugs and alcohol, or that these children were exposed to lead paint in foster homes. Some of these answers may be a part of the true answer. Many adopted kids with learning disabilities do have some of the indicators for attention deficit disorder (ADD) or attention deficit hyperactivity disorder (ADHD).

What is more than clear, though, is that all of the children who are adopted, or who are foster children, or who are in other complex family situations and working hard to make sense of these complexities, have emotional obstacles to dealing with these challenges and divided loyalties. This extra emotional work—what I would call a normative crisis under challenging circumstances—influences the learning styles of these children. We have found, over the years, that it's very important to pay attention to these issues and to begin to work with the children to address what is blocking them from learning.

Tony's story   This was made quite clear to me in a session once with an eight-year-old boy named Tony, whose short life had been disrupted many times. His was a complex case, because he had been taken care of by family members while his mother was in and out of drug rehabilitation and then had been placed in three different foster homes for various reasons. He obviously had experienced much loss.

Tony had been placed in resource rooms at school and was getting special help for his serious learning disabilities. He was having social problems as well as behavior problems in school. Tony was extremely bright, and I found this little boy incredibly insightful. One day, I was playing blocks with him, trying to get him to do a little bit of math indirectly when he burst into tears and said, "I can't do subtraction. As soon as they say 'take away,' it makes me feel really sad." This was one of my saddest and most profound experiences working with children; I understood that Tony's losses had blocked him from doing math from the moment "taking away" became a part of it. He wasn't going to learn in a class that was about loss.

It took a concerted effort with Tony's teachers and his family and with Tony himself to better understand the posttraumatic issues of this child. We began to acknowledge that there was a need to learn addition before taking on subtraction. Tony also benefited from what I call narrative therapy and was eventually able, through recovered photographs and stories, to make a narrative of his life. For adopted people it is often true that other people hold much of one's story; without authoring and holding one's own story, it is hard to feel in control of one's own life. Tony began to feel he had more control over the story of his life and more control over the memories of what had happened— some bad, but some very good—and all of them until now lost along with the bad. As soon as we were doing addition and not subtraction, Tony's ability to concentrate, to be available to learn in general, and his math skills in particular, increased, and he was able to do much better.

At least two of the foster families Tony had been in had been important and good families for him. We have a habit in this culture of cutting people off, and this carries over into our foster care system. When these placements are done, they're done; a child is expected to move on and never to see those people he's lived with again. Tony's family was willing to form a connection with some of these people, though, and to reweave some of the positive people back into his life. That was an important move that had a strong impact on him.

❖

Some other school-related issues for adopted children are equally tied to a particular subject. An inordinate number of adoptees we see are either brilliant in history or they *hate* it. I've talked to many children about this, and the common thread is that they know virtually nothing about their own history, so they are either ravenous to know everything about everyone else's history, or just don't see any point in it.

Several years ago, I was at a private psychiatric hospital with a day school to do a consult. The family I was seeing there had an adopted child who was in the day program, and she had been released from one of her classes to come to the consult. She said, "Oh! I planned this so carefully: I'm out of history class." I just laughed; her reaction is so typical for many adopted children.

Ryan's story　　I once had a client named Ryan, an adopted boy who was a gifted English student, who used to write fabulous papers and bring them in for me to read. But, suddenly in the eighth grade, he was failing English. In November of that year, his parents brought him in for a "checkup." I sent the parents out to the waiting room and asked him, "Ryan, what's going on? When did you all of a sudden start to fail English?" He said, "October 4th." That was the day he'd been assigned a book about a foster child. Ryan had been in foster care until he was eighteen months old, when he was adopted by his family. He had never talked about his foster family, and his adoptive family had never thought to bring it up as an issue.

The book brought up many emotional issues for him, and he couldn't finish it. Nor could he write the book report, and he was given an "F." This failing grade triggered a downward spiral, until Ryan figured that, since he was on his way to flunking English, he might as well not do anything else.

Kenny's story　　I have one final story having to do with specific school subjects. Kenny was eight years old when he was assigned a geography project on his birth country, Korea. He came home from school one day and said to his mother, as he drank his juice and ate his cookies, "Do you know how many people there are in Seoul, where I was born?" She said, "No, tell me," and he told her how many billions. Then he said, "Do you know how many people there are in the whole country of Korea?" and she said, "No," and he told her how many trillions. And then he sat and stared out the window and eventually said, "I understand how you told me that my birth mother could not take care of me, but what was wrong with all of those other billions of people?" A single school assignment had underlined for Kenny his feelings of rejection, not only by his birth family, but by his extended family and birth culture as well.

Schools need to be sensitive to the impact of some assignments on some children. If math or history or English or geography present a problem for some adopted children, the family tree assignment—an almost universal project in the primary grades—creates a huge dilemma for all adopted children. And adopted children are not the only ones for whom this can create inner conflict; this is also true for foster children, stepchildren, and children in guardianship.

When my own daughter was in the third grade, she had a wonderful teacher who was beginning a unit called Backyard History. This curriculum began with the child's own family history and then moved into community history. I realized that the family tree part of this assignment caused a dilemma for most kids with complex families. At this primary-school age and stage of development, the children would be likely to feel they needed to decide which family tree was *right*. Is it cheating to chart your adoptive family as your roots—where you began—if it isn't the truth? The inner turmoil this creates for many kids is not usually visible.

My daughter's teacher wondered along with me about how it might lessen the turmoil for some kids to talk about potential problems with the assignment in advance. I spent time in the classroom going over the fact that not everyone has just a family tree; that some people have whole orchards. There are kids in stepfamilies; there are those who have foster families; there are some who have adoptive families and birth families. This was the beginning of a curriculum I've developed—I call it the family orchard—for blended families, including adoptive families. Unlike the traditional family tree assignment, the family orchard allows children to show the numerous trees that contributed to their being. It acknowledges the fact that adoptive families are not totally unlike a stepfamily, or a foster family, in that they are complex; there is more than one set of mothers and fathers. Even if a child does not know his or her birth parents, the family orchard helps to acknowledge what the child essentially knows: there is another mother and father even if they are not the parents. They are there. *They are real.*

This inclusive approach also makes it unnecessary to pull adopted kids out of classrooms to do special groups for them. At this age, they are most often quite aware of the fact that they are different and they do not need to have this magnified any further, or to feel set apart. It's important to keep it their choice to talk with peers about being adopted. Being sent to a group identifies something about them that they may prefer to keep private.

One last school issue that we commonly see for adopted children is daydreaming. Adoption is an archetypal theme. We find it in mythology, biblical stories, and fairy tales. It is a theme that occurs again and again in children's literature and film. When adopted children watch these movies or read these stories in school, they have a tendency to identify with them and to lose focus as they daydream. Daydreaming is a normal occurrence for people who are kept from knowing the truths of their lives and who are living with fantasy. It is a way to reframe things that are hard to understand and to compensate for things that are painful. For many school-aged adopted children, daydreaming is a very understandable and necessary strategy for doing the extra work of forming identity. Daydreaming, though, is often taken as a symptom of attention deficit disorder or attention deficit hyperactive disorder; it is in fact one of the many indicators that leads to the diagnosis of ADD. There are many children who do have this real disorder, and it is important in these cases to find the appropriate behavioral or pharmacological treatments. But, for adopted children, and for some other children in complex or difficult situations, the daydreaming or distracted air is not always an indicator of ADD.

Too often, teachers seem to be making diagnoses and suggesting medications and treatments to parents. This is inappropriate and uneth-

ical, and it is one of the reasons I feel the curriculum in schools of education must include information concerning the special circumstances of
adoptive families.

Anger, control, and transitions

Reggie's story　A little boy I worked with a couple of years ago was four
years old when his parents adopted another child. Reggie's parents involved him in the adoption of their second child, and he learned more
concretely about adoption as he observed his sister being "dopted." At
that point, he began to ask many questions about himself. His adoptive
parents were able to explain things to him clearly and concretely. They
were comfortable doing this and they were glad to have the opportunity
to begin to talk openly with Reggie about his own adoption.

　　Soon afterward, though, he started to have problems in school
with other children, and he was having difficulty falling asleep. His parents were worried about these new behaviors. They thought perhaps
some of it was because he had a new sibling, but they wondered whether
it might be developmental—or did it have to do with adoption?

　　The family came into my office and I asked Reggie why he
thought he was having such a hard time. He said that there were rules in
his house and one rule was that if he played in the backyard, he had to
play within view of the kitchen window so that his mom could see him.
If she *couldn't* see him, she either got all worried, or she got angry and
punished him for not keeping the rule.

　　I asked if he thought that was an okay rule, and he said yes.

　　I asked why, then, was he having such a hard time? Reggie said,
"My other mother doesn't see me and so she must be either very upset
and scared, or very, very angry at me. Mothers get upset or mad when
they can't see you sometimes. I miss my other mother and I think she
really misses me and she wonders where I am. I feel bad for her not
knowing where I am."

　　Reggie's adoptive parents were understandably moved and upset. They had done such a good job of explaining about his birth mother
in a positive and loving way, and Reggie was such a sensitive and empathetic boy, that he really was concerned for her. In the time that fol-

lowed, we had several family sessions. We talked about adoption and about Reggie's feelings.

Reggie's mother wanted to go to the agency to try to get some information about the birth mother—about the birth parents. She felt that if Reggie really wanted this, she was willing to do it.

At the time his parents adopted Reggie, they had wanted only to have their baby. They didn't care to learn much about the birth parents, and they surely did not want to meet them. Now that they were completely secure in their being Reggie's parents, they heard his questions and understood his needs and wished they had access to the birth parents, or at least to the birth mother.

Reggie's had been a closed adoption from a traditional agency, which said that contact would not be within the rights of the birth mother. The agency was unequivocal about this. Reggie's mother didn't know what to do, but she felt that if she were truly the parent and had parental rights, she and her husband should be able to make decisions that were in Reggie's best interest. Reggie's mother asked if the agency would act as intermediary, if she could send pictures and letters, as she now saw happening in many semi-open adoptions. The agency said that she was welcome to send anything and that they would put it in the file, but that they would not contact the birth mother, as that was not their policy.

In the course of my work with Reggie, I began to have him dictate some letters to his birth mother and to draw some pictures for her. He began to be able to say some of the things to her that he needed to say. His parents came in after he had done a series of these and we showed the picutures and letters to them. Reggie said one of them was private, so that one was sealed. The others, he said, they could read. He wanted them to be put in a place where they could be given to his birth mother when he did find her.

This began to make him feel more in control and more connected to his birth mother. It was terribly important for him to have some outward way to make concrete sense of these two mother-people. Thus far, he has not brought up his birth father. That often happens later, along with questions about possible siblings.

✛

Most of the children we see at our clinic who are ages four to eight have particular issues with anger. There is a great deal of loss in adoption, and feelings of loss often manifest themselves as anger. People, from the outside, see adoption as a very positive occasion, and, in fact, it is. The birth parents and the adoptive parents, however, have most often gone through a great deal of loss and sadness to get to an adoption decision, and that loss and sadness is passed on directly or indirectly to the child as an underlying fact of adoption. We have learned in recent years that it does not help the child in the long run to disguise the reality of any situation; that it is better to tell the truths and to help the child learn to cope with them.

It is much easier to teach a child who is angry how to deal with his anger than to comfort a child who is severely depressed. Anger is dynamic—it moves. Depression can seem more like paralysis. There is reason for an adopted child or foster child to be angry, and the best gift is to set the limits and to teach them ways to deal with anger. It is a real emotion and one that's warranted under the circumstances.

Control is another prevalent issue for young adopted children. After all, if you'd been separated, moved, had your name changed— your whole life changed in an instant—might you not worry about control? Adopted children know it's not just a fantasy that things can happen to you. They know you *can* lose parents. You *can* be taken and moved. These things happened at least once to every child who is adopted. As a result they often need to know *everything* that is going to happen and to have it explained many times. They may have difficulty at night falling asleep. This difficulty is not simply a ploy to stay up later and later (although this may enter the picture), it's an expression of the fact that when you go to sleep, you lose control.

Some adopted children seem to adapt quickly to nearly any situation: it is a resilient skill. Internally, however, the transitions are very difficult.

An adopted child who is about to visit foster parents or birth parents or her country of origin may need a great deal of reassurance from the adoptive parents that she is not going to be left there. For an adopted child, being left at school—being left anywhere—can often be fraught with the feelings of loss and the separation issues that are just beneath the surface.

I have a friend with a young adopted son who loves his summer camp. He talks about it all fall and winter and spring. He tells everyone stories about his friends from camp and his exciting experiences. Yet, every year it takes him about two weeks to get himself psychologically ready to go. He picks fights with his parents and at-home friends. He struggles with his divided loyalty at liking his life away from his home. He needs time and space to work out his transition and to believe that it is okay. By now my friend and her son have learned to recongnize the little dance that starts whenever he is beginning something new. I've talked to grown-up adopted people many times about this issue, and many of them still need to go through a difficult internal adjustment to change. Most adults have developed the necessary strategies for coping with transitions, but cope we must.

All of these things—anger, the need for control, difficulty making transitions—are of course a normal part of life with young children. For adopted children, however, these issues are often magnified. Parents, teachers, and others who work with children must understand the issues and be compassionate—and firm—when separation and loss are the underlying themes.

Chapter 4
The adopted preadolescent (eight to twelve years) and early adolescent (twelve to sixteen years)

As they approach adolescence, many children turn inward and do not wish to talk, especially to their parents, about how they feel regarding many subjects, certainly including adoption. But this stage—what is called latency in children—is the very best time to talk to and to work with children who are struggling with their feelings about adoption, before the onslaught of even more complex adolescent issues.

Often parents and professionals ask themselves, "Does she ever think about adoption," or "Does he ever talk about adoption?" The answer usually seems to be no, and everyone thinks that all is well. These are the wrong questions to be asking. Children at this stage are concrete thinkers. They do not sit around thinking about the concept of adoption. If asked about adoption they think of the legal fact, or of something barely related to themselves and to their own feelings.

A ten-year-old girl whose parents have done an admirable job helping her know what adoption means and who've given her the tools to talk about adoption wrote a wonderful poem. I love this poem because, without ever mentioning the word adoption, it shows how Julia's life as an adopted person feels and how it has taken shape in her innermost thoughts.

Me

Before I was born
God had a plan
For me and my surroundings.
He gave me two mothers

And sent me two fathers,
And sighed, "Oh me, oh my.
This baby, this child.
What shall I do?"
And He wrote down,
Three sisters, two brothers.

He wrote down,
Girl, not boy,
Asian, nothing else
And He added a few lies.
But then he made me
A Good Child.
And gave me love, talent and peace.

Before I was born,
God had a plan for
My two mothers and two fathers.
He gave them mistakes,
He wrote down joy.
And sent them the gift of talent.

God wrote down sadness,
Loss and fear.
He gave me an empty hole.
Inside that hole,
Little by little
Happiness begins to form
A star.
And in that star,
He gave me hope,
That I must use always.

Across the sea,
My first mother dwells.
Here at home,
My mother lives.
God made it that way

I believe.
He wrote down
Sad and scared.
But then He gave me the star,
Of hope and
An unfinished book, laid
Aside.

Julia Wisbach, age 10

Julia holds her birth parents and her adoptive parents together in her mind; she is able to make sense of her connections to her past as well as to her present. She is fortunate to have parents who have supported her need to keep her respect for the parents who gave her birth. Julia and her adoptive family have gone to Korea and have met her birth family, and one of Julia's birth sisters has come to spend a summer vacation with her and her adoptive parents, who are now like an aunt and uncle to her sister. Families can expand in fulfilling and lovely ways through adoption.

The fear of losing a child keeps some parents from being open to information that so often can help a child build a sense of identity and self-esteem.

Katie's story   I once had a phone call from an irate adoptive parent who had received a call from their adoption agency twelve years after their daughter, whom I will call Katie, had been placed with them. They felt invaded by the call and wanted to talk about it.

When they arrived in my office, the parents explained that Katie's birth mother had recently written to the agency. She'd left a letter in the file for the parents and wanted them to know, as soon as possible, that the birth father had recently died of a genetic illness that had been unknown at the time of the placement.

The birth mother wanted to have some correspondence and connection with the twelve-year-old and was willing to send pictures and to use the agency as an intermediary. This had not been the plan at the time of adoption. The adoptive parents felt shocked, first, by the death of the birth father and the possibility that his illness might be carried by their daughter and, second, by the invasive feeling of having the birth mother appear out of nowhere.

After some counseling, the parents came to feel that this was a very loving thing for the birth mother to have done. With this understanding, they could tell Katie's pediatrician and they could be sure to do everything to detect and prevent the illness.

Still the parents felt that they should wait until Katie was about eighteen to tell her any of this. I suggested that eighteen is actually a hard time for young adults to take on new information about their identity, especially if it has been kept from them until then. They are ready to leave home to go to college, and there is the threat of losing an even greater connection to their parents for not having entrusted this information to them earlier. I also suggested that it might be best for Katie to have the loving support of her adoptive family as she worked out the feelings she had about all of this information. At age eighteen or twenty-one, most young people are not in the supportive environment of home, but rather at college or on their own.

The parents considered all of this and left my office. Our consultation was over. They had driven for four hours to come in to talk and were not going to come back for regular sessions, so I knew I might never know the outcome. A few months later, though, this letter arrived.

> *Dear Dr. Pavao:*
>
> *We wanted to let you know how much you helped us with a difficult decision.*
>
> *When we left your office, we were confident in our decision to tell Katie about the death of her birth father. We did, and she seemed to handle it just fine. You also advised us to let her birth mother write to Katie. She did, and Katie was happy to receive the letter and the pictures of her birth parents as children. She looks just like her birth father's sister!*
>
> *Katie has not decided to write back to her birth mother yet. We think that she may send a birthday card in July. This gives her time to digest this new information. We have had her speak with a neighbor who has two open adoptions about how she feels and the neighbor thinks that she seems very comfortable with this information and knowing more about herself.*
>
> *We feel sure that someday our daughter will meet her birth*

*mother. We are hopeful, because of ongoing letters, that the meeting will
be a happy one.*

Thank you for your help.

I feel very fortunate to know the outcome of Katie's parents' decision. Most adoption professionals have no further connection with a
family after an adoption is legalized. This is especially true of judges and
attorneys. They often have no idea what the ongoing issues are likely to
be or how an adoption might have been handled differently at the outset
to prevent pain and sorrow later.

Ricardo's story   One of the stories that touches my heart most is that of
a young man who was adopted at about age five from an orphanage in
Colombia. His adoptive parents went to Colombia and stayed in a hotel
while they awaited the processing of papers. They finally got their little
boy and brought him back to their home. They decided to name him
Trevor, a family name.

Trevor adapted and fit in. He did have the expected language
problem that slowed him down in school, and he got extra help for this.
He liked sports and was kept very busy and seemed quite happy.

At age thirteen, he attempted suicide. Upon his release from the
hospital, the family was referred to me for family therapy. I sat in a room
with a severely depressed young man and his nervous parents. I asked
the parents first to tell me the story of Trevor's adoption. I then asked
what was going on around the time of the attempted suicide. The parents both said "nothing," that "everything seemed fine." I probed some
more and the father said that they were in the process of having Trevor
become a naturalized citizen, but that couldn't be the problem! I asked
the parents to wait outside and I spent time alone with Trevor.

He was deeply depressed. I asked if we could think together about
anything that would make him want to live. Would he want to go back
to Colombia? He looked at me candidly and said, "Joyce, you do not understand. I do not live. I died when I was five years old. I had another
name, another language, another family, and then I became this person
that I am trying to be. I can't try any longer." I sat and listened. I asked,
"What do you call yourself in your head, when you talk to yourself?"

He said, "Ricardo."

I asked if he thought his parents would give him back his name and he responded, "You don't understand. I love my parents. I don't want to hurt them." I suggested that the suicide attempt had hurt them, and that after weathering that they were probably able to withstand the idea of a name change! I asked him what else he would like. He said, "I'd like to be around people who look like me. I am in a white family and an all white school and neighborhood and there is no one like me." He said that he didn't want to be a U.S. citizen: "I lost my country, my language, my people, and I don't want to lose anything else. That is all that I have."

I asked if we could invite his parents back in and tell them what we had talked about. He said, "You tell them," and so I did. When the parents heard about his name they cried. His mother said, "I wanted you to have a family name so that you would feel that you belonged. I never wanted to make you feel bad." Ricardo then put his arm around his mom's shoulders and told her that it had been hard for him to get used to a new name, and he knew she would slip too, but that it was okay.

We then talked about citizenship, and his father explained how important U.S. citizenship could be to him. He suggested that if Ricardo got his name back, he would have something from his past, and that at age twenty-one he could choose to be a citizen of anywhere.

I brought up the issue of Ricardo being a minority of one in his world. I asked if the parents would consider moving to a more diverse community a few towns away. (I was stretching a bit, I knew, but wanted to introduce the idea.) The father said the market was bad. After all, they had a huge property in Dover and stables and all and why would they move? I then suggested that they look into private schools with a commitment to diversity. Not just diversity of students, but faculty members who would be mirrors for Ricardo as well. I asked Ricardo if this would do. He said, "I guess so."

Ricardo went on to a high school with a diverse student body and faculty and had a good experience there. He studied and relearned Spanish. He and his father took a bicycle trip through Colombia when he graduated from high school, and they went back to visit the orphanage and to find out if there was any information about his birth family. There was. Ricardo did no more searching on that trip. He went to college and decided to spend his junior year in Colombia; he wanted to be in an American program, but in Colombia.

He felt worried that he wouldn't fit in there either. While in Colombia he found his birth family and discovered some difficult things—

that there had been violence and poverty. Ricardo realized he had real memories of these things that he had felt were just "bad thoughts." He had in fact witnessed violence, and had been subjected to it. This discovery, painful though it was, actually validated Ricardo's sense of himself and allowed him to go forward. Ricardo went on to law school and majored in international law and human rights, and he is now a champion for the children of the world.

I wanted to tell Ricardo's story because he is an example of the fragility of a child who is uprooted and the danger of moving a child without thinking of the long-term consequences. When Ricardo first came into my office he felt dead. He was indeed in danger of dying at age thirteen by his own hand. He needed to have his past brought back to him in order to feel that he might have a future.

Adolescent issues

Adolescence is complicated for everyone, but it can be especially complicated for children who are adopted.

Some of the famous psychoanalysts—Margaret Mahler, Edith Jacobson—have shown that what happens in one's early life, between birth and age three, gets reworked during adolescence. If what happened in one's early life was to be separated from one's birth parents, placed in a foster home, separated from one's foster family and then placed in an adoptive family, then that is an extremely complex experience to rework.

During adolescence divided loyalty is a recurring theme for adopted children. They have a hard time feeling uncomplicatedly loyal to their adoptive family while they are coming to an understanding of who and what their birth family is and sorting out their feelings about them. The traditional approach to adoption, which suggests that we forget all about the family of origin and genetic connections, does not allow an adopted child or adolescent to make sense of *both* sets of *real* parents. This causes a very real and predictable divided loyalty and conflict about identity.

It is during early adolescence that adoptive parents most often hear the words "you are not my 'real' mother and father." This is because the child is processing the complex idea of adoption and knows concretely, for the first time, that the adoptive parents are not the parents who gave birth to her or from whom her genetic makeup came. Adolescents understand that *real* means genuine. Biologically they are real human beings because of the real parents who gave them birth. In processing this, an angry comment about what their parents are *not* shows that there is some internal sorting out being done.

Meanwhile, all but overwhelming changes are going on physiologically and hormonally for these young people. Apart from the first three years of a child's life, adolescence is when the most drastic development occurs. The hormonal changes, the mood swings, are of course legendary. Young people are beginning to do some abstract thinking. These changes also often bring on a crisis of personal loss. If an adopted adolescent has issues about loss, and if she has little or no information about her origins, then the loss of her former self—her child self—is painful in a way that it is not for other adolescents.

In early adolescence loss of childhood *is* the big issue. For all children this is difficult. Many of the children we see who are twelve or thirteen are sucking their thumbs on their parents' laps one minute and the next minute pushing their parents away.

For a child who has a foundation of loss, then, the transition to adolescence becomes that much more complicated. So many adoptees have a more challenging adolescence because of these issues, and they often begin having problems in school—attention issues and processing problems that we will discuss specifically later.

The following poem gives a window on the conflict and confusion a child feels as he grapples as an adolescent with losses in his early life.

So Many Years

So many cold winters
and hot summers
have passed through my life
and still I try to picture
your faces in my mind
I was separated from you
at the age of three
Where did you put me

on the streets to die
or on the streets to be found
What happened to you
Did you really die
or was it just a cover up
Was I not good enough
or were you not good enough
I want to know, but how
can you hear me crying
Would you even care
If I found you
Should I be mad or sad
Maybe God can help
I need to know who you are
Don't you care who I am
Do you wonder what I look like
Maybe it's a good thing
I did not stay around
but why
All I need is a picture
Something that will stay
in my memory for always

I'm fine where I am now
I love them and I love you
So many nights I stay awake
trying to figure out why
what happened to you
what happened to me
It hurts so much sometimes
Someday this will all
come to an end somehow.

Sam Sulahian, age 14

Another huge issue during adolescence is sexuality. The messages about sexuality that surround virtually all adolescents in late-twentieth-century culture are blatant and damaging enough, but many adopted children are especially sensitive to them because of their identification with what they imagine about their birth parents' sexuality.

The assumptions and stereotypical messages a child absorbs about birth parents, often shaped by the media, are: *Your birth father was some fly-by-night, got someone pregnant, and disappeared. Your birth mother, obviously, was sleeping with people and wasn't married or she would have been able to keep you.* It doesn't matter what story the adoptive parents tell, society has its own myths and misconceptions surrounding adoption. Our culture's image of who these children are affects their identity a great deal. It affects their thinking about sexuality, bringing up questions like, what does it mean that my adoptive parents are infertile. Does it mean they don't have sex? How does it mean they can't have babies?

When parents are in their own pain due to infertility, it is sometimes difficult to discuss thoughts and feelings about sex and procreation. It is no surprise that the adopted adolescent's self-image as the product of illicit/uncondoned sex coupled with the misconception of infertile parents as sexless is tough to reconcile. It is no surprise that a large number of adolescent adoptees become, or make someone else, pregnant. They are trying to be like their birth parents and trying to make sense of the little information they have about where they come from.

Penny Callan Partridge's *My Dog Story* is a wonderful reminder of this:

> In my last year of college, I got engaged, broke the engagement, and filled out an application for the Peace Corps. Among other things, I wanted new vistas.
>
> And I got them. I was sent to a "bush" school in Nigeria. I saw people DANCE up to each other as their way of saying, "Nice to see you!" When the rain ran under my door, I went out and dug a trench to make it go around my house. I learned I could easily do without electricity or running water. And I had my first dog.
>
> A volunteer on his way home had given me his dog, Kai Kai, named after the local palm wine brandy. Kai Kai was part border collie, part something else, and pregnant. One night around 3:00 A.M., Kai Kai came to get me out of bed. She nudged me into my biggest chair and climbed on my lap. She then gave birth to eight puppies.
>
> Each puppy sliding out of Kai Kai looked like a wet chipmunk in

plastic wrap. Kai Kai would get each one cleaned up and settled, and then we would go back into a kind of embrace to wait for the next contractions.

As a child, I had been upset that my parents insisted on having our cats "fixed." I had so much wanted our household—probably our history—to include pregnancy and birth. I couldn't have said that I felt cut off from my own birth, but I did feel deprived of any direct association with birth. I felt exiled from the whole world of reproduction.

With Kai Kai giving birth in my arms, I reentered that world. I began thinking that no less than these puppies, I myself must have slid out of a warm, wet body. Was that body still alive somewhere? And wouldn't the woman whose body it was want to know a person who had entered the world through HER BODY?

I left Nigeria as the region I was in tried to give birth to itself, as the Independent Republic of Biafra—an effort that never succeeded. A few weeks later, I crossed the San Francisco Bay to the Children's Home Society in Oakland, where my parents had picked me up.

That day, for the first time in my life, I said out loud that I was interested in meeting the woman who had given birth to me. I didn't actually meet her for nine more years. And I never got to give birth myself. But "birth" had been given to me by Kai Kai.

It is so important to normalize birth and life for all children, to give them a sense that they are a part of the universe, a part of the world. Many adoptees feel as if they came from outer space because there is no story of their birth, only the wonderful story of their adoption. Each child also needs a story of his or her birth—a sense of a beginning and of being human.

✢

Erik Erikson states that identity formation is a most important issue during adolescence. I have been a student of Erikson's work since I was first able to be part of a small seminar that he taught during my studies at Harvard. My research was on identity and adoption, and I told Erikson that I was so glad to talk to him about identity because of his reputation as "the Father of Identity." He said, "No, I'm the Father of Identity Confusion."

He himself never met his birth father; he was half adopted. Erikson's birth mother married his much-loved adoptive father when Erikson was three. When he tried to search for his birth father, after his mother died, his uncles refused to tell him anything and he had no way to find out who his birth father was.

When Erikson came to this country, he made up his own surname. He named himself "Erik's son" as a way of taking control of his life, of becoming his own father, since his own name was all he knew, all he had with which to form a connection. It was not that he did not love and cherish his adoptive father, but that he needed to feel his place, his genetic connection to the world.

Issues of identity are important to adopted children even if they grow up in a family that sort of looks like them. Even if they are in a family of the same ethnic background, they still don't look much like everyone else at the big family Thanksgiving dinner. During latency and early adolescence, children begin to notice more and more how different they look and how different (they think) they feel.

I often ask a question when I'm talking with people about adoption: What would it be like if you did not know another human being *on this earth* who was related to you?

Stop and think.

Most people say that they can't imagine. They might say they *wish* they weren't related to some of their kin, but they know their relatives and know of more through family stories and pictures passed down from generation to generation. They can see likenesses when they look around at a family gathering. They can compare the crook in the little finger that is a family trait or laugh at the dimple that appears on all the girls in the family.

When your adoption is closed, and you have no knowledge of siblings or other relatives, it is almost as if you are the only person in the world. You have no genetic connections. You have loving and wonderful relationships, you have your adoptive family and you love them, but unless you are placed with a sibling, or have some information about your birth parents, or know someone related to you by birth, you have no genetic connections. This sense of disconnection is hard even for same-race, same-ethnicity adoptees, so it is even more pronounced for international and transracial adoptees.

Many adolescents are not dealing with these facts and feelings concretely. They are not thinking about all this in a defined way, and they often will not admit to anyone that they are thinking about these lonely issues at all.

In our therapy with adolescents—and our largest number of clients are adolescent adoptees and their families—we see the family first. I always begin with "Let's Make a Deal" with the parents. The deal is that anything the kids say in therapy is confidential, unless it's that they are going to hurt themselves or someone else. However, anything that the parents tell me—whether I see them without the child, see one of them individually, or they call me between sessions—is *not* confidential.

Parents always ask, "Well, why?" I tell them it's because these kids have issues of trust. Their very first situation in life was to be disrupted. Trust is a hard thing for them to develop, and it's important to gain a sense of trust with these children if one is to work with them. They do not need to have the feeling that you, the clinician, is just another adult siding with their parents. We have seen that our "Let's Make a Deal" arrangement, which is one parents and children are well aware of, can help.

There are *enough* secrets in the lives of adoptees. They do not need secrets within therapy as well.

When I am working alone with the kids, the word "adoption" may *never* come up. We don't talk about it directly very often, and usually only if the child brings it up. We talk about all kinds of surrounding issues, but not necessarily using the word. Kids often feel more comfortable talking about adoption indirectly, as if it's not about themselves. At certain times, they need that distance.

With this in mind, a few years ago I developed what I call soap opera therapy. Several of the adoptees I was seeing were watching soap operas, and I realized I had four or five kids who were coming in each week and talking about one particular soap.

I had my daughter teach me how to tape television shows, and I started staying up late at night occasionally to watch this particular soap opera. (Once you get the gist, believe me, you don't have to watch every episode to stay *au courant*.)

I was amazed: there were five intersecting adoption stories going on in this one soap opera. There was a girl who had searched for and found her birth father and was looking for her birth mother; there was a guy who had found out he was adopted and wasn't who he thought he was; and there were three other adoption stories actively worked into the plot.

Soap opera therapy became a truly useful model. We often talked about soap operas for about fifteen minutes and then we'd move on to what it would be like to be in the position of the people in the show. We began to get to the issues of adoption and how they related to these kids. I still often rely on soap opera therapy as a way to begin a dialogue about adoption and what it means to a child.

A few years ago I was in Los Angeles, and was introduced to the head writer of *Days of Our Lives*. I was invited to do a little consulting about adoption issues for the show, only to find out that the head writer was, herself, an adoptee. She was sixty-three years old and had been placed for adoption privately in the South. There was no way of her ever finding out anything about her birth parents, but she had always written about her fantasies. Many of her scripts for *Days of Our Lives* and other shows contained adoption search and fantasy themes. It was moving to me to learn how this writer used stories to heal and to tell her how much therapy she was providing others!

❖

We see a fairly large number of adopted children who "run away" during their adolescence. What they are truly doing is *running toward*. These are children who are trying to search for other families—trying to see what it is like to be in a different family. They are dealing with their divided loyalty toward their birth and adoptive parents, and some are reworking the many moves that were inflicted on them at very early ages. They are trying to figure out where they belong. They are trying to figure out where they come from. They are trying to be active, not passive, in choosing a family to identify with at this difficult age and stage of development. These children are in the throes of a search. It may not be a concrete search for their actual birth parents, but it is nevertheless an internal search for self and for identity.

It is obviously upsetting for adoptive parents to have a child run away. In many instances, runaways must be referred to the state Department of Social Services, and this is not in the best interest of the family— especially if the people involved will not be able to help because they do not understand that this is not like any other running away.

These children are not running *far* away; very often they are running to a friend's house. They are trying to figure out what is happening in their life. They are trying to rework something from the past. This is a time when services are needed for the family and for the child. It is not in the best interest of a child to be disconnected from his or her adoptive family. This is because all of the child's family connections, through birth and adoption, need to be seen as integral. The child should not be made to disregard his identity as belonging to an adoptive family at this difficult time, any more than he should be told to cut off emotional ties to the idea of his birth family.

Many professionals who get involved at this time either tend to blame the child or to blame the parents. Blame is not what is needed. These reactions are not the fault of the parents or the child. They are the fault of a system that does not explain and allow the concrete and relevant truth to be known and legally accepted. This is a child born of another mother and father who could not parent him. They are still a part of who the child is genetically and they hold a part of his story.

This is also the child of adoptive parents who have been the only *parents* to the child, and who have given him love and care and all of their values and beliefs. This is a child with a blended history who should be respected enough to have been given all of the truths as he grew. If this was done by the system, the child would not be in such conflict during this difficult stage of adolescence.

This is a crisis of search, and it is an opportunity to help families to communicate and to understand what is happening. The most important thing is to keep the connections. So many connections have already been lost, especially for children who have orphanages or foster homes as part of their history.

Sometimes, though, things get so confusing, and the anger and ambivalence a child feels about parents in general are directed completely toward the adoptive parents, especially the mother. There are some adolescent adoptees who act out intensely, almost abusively, to their adoptive parents. When this happens, the child and the family may need time apart.

At this point, the child (and family) may be better off with the child at a boarding school, or in another family setting chosen by both parents and child. If this can be done without external intervention, it will feel like a more normal and in-control choice for the whole family.

For instance, there may be an aunt in another state who can take the child and have her attend school there for awhile.

This mutually agreed on time away can be a creative and safe way to provide another setting for the child while she is working through issues of divided loyalty without permanently harming the precious and important ties to the adoptive family.

Leaving home for any of us is not easy. But for these kids, adopted adolescents who have issues of loss and of disconnection, leaving home is extremely difficult. One way to deal with this is by attempting *never* to leave home. (This is addressed in chapter 5.)

✢

Along with problems about loss and leave-taking, one of the issues that confronts us over and over again is that most adoptees are adopted from a lower socioeconomic background *into* a middle-class or upper-middle-class family: that is the way adoption works in this country for the most part. Very often as adopted children grow up and begin to ask questions about where they came from, they are told, "Your birth mother was very young and very poor and therefore she could not raise you. That is the reason you were placed for adoption." That is the *simple* story many kids are told. What people do not understand is the impact that story has on the inner life of the adopted person. If that is all you know about your birth parent, that is information you become extremely loyal to. You become a champion of the underprivileged, or you become one yourself.

I cannot tell you how many parents come into therapy complaining that their kids are hanging around with the wrong crowd. Many of these adoptees are simply being loyal to what they believe to be the place and the people they came from. They are drawn to people they think they belong to. These affiliations often make parents of a higher socioeconomic background upset and afraid for their children. The more the parents say, "Your friends are no good," or, "You shouldn't be hanging out in the projects," the more angry the adoptee gets, because in her heart and mind she is thinking, "That is my birth mother you're talking about. That is who I *really* am. So you're talking about me, you're not talking about my friends."

Parents and professionals need to understand what the adopted person is thinking adoption means at all stages of development. Communication—dialogue about the socioeconomic issue and so many others—is essential to educating everyone involved and clarifying their feelings.

Rachel's story   One of the families I worked with was dealing with a different but equally powerful set of confused messages. The family was a Jewish, religious one that had adopted three children, two girls and a boy. The older two, a girl and a boy, had had problems growing up, but nothing too difficult. The youngest girl had been the perfect child—until adolescence, when she had started acting out all over the place. The parents came to see me wondering if Rachel's problems had anything to do with adoption. They didn't think so, but someone had suggested they explore this possibility.

I always ask the parents during the first session to tell the story of the adoption. The children invariably sit on the edge of their seats for this. If you are an adoptee, as you hear the story about what happened at the time of your adoption, the story *changes* over time; there are new adjectives, new elaborations, different moods. It is painful for adoptees that they do not hold their own story, that others hold many of the secrets and many of the pieces of it. And so they sit on the edge of their seats: there may be new evidence this time.

Rachel's parents, though, had very little to tell. They said that all they were told by the agency at the time was that Rachel's birth mother was Protestant and that she played the piano and sang. Such scraps of information—some true and some fabricated—were typical of adoptions in the 1940s, '50s, and even in some cases the '80s and '90s. A few words concerning the mother's ethnic or religious background and perhaps her hobby was all the information you got.

At the time of the adoption, as I've discussed in chapter 2, many adoptive parents are tired of infertility issues and of home studies, and exhausted by the emotional roller coaster of the adoption process. They simply want their baby so that they can begin a family. At this point, some need the baby to be "all theirs." Often, they honestly don't want to know very much about the baby's birth parents or life before them. What they don't know becomes a concern to them only later. As the child grows and asks questions, and the parents *know* now that they are the true parents, they begin to wish they had more to share with their child about his or her background. Even when the parents really do not have answers, the child feels that the parents are withholding—that they do know and are not telling. Lack of information makes victims of the parents as well as of the child.

Rachel's parents started talking about things happening currently in the family. One of the problems was that Rachel was acting out very dangerously, and they were worried about her. She was truant from school. She was sexually active. She was using drugs. One of their biggest concerns was that she was dating non-Jewish boys. Rachel thought they were crazy . . . she wasn't dating anyone, but she *was* sleeping with almost every boy in her high school. The parents were terribly hurt and worried and angry about all of this.

We talked about the parents' beliefs and how important it was for them to hold these beliefs and to convey them to their daughter and to all their children.

Rachel talked about the fact that she thought they were wrong. Why should she exclude someone if she liked him because he was not of the same religion?

I asked the parents, as innocently as possible, "Do you think the non-Jewish boyfriends have anything to do with the fact that her birth mother was Protestant?" There was a long silence. Rachel eventually shook her head and said, "Yeah. If they don't like people who aren't Jewish, they must not like *me* very much."

The parents were shocked, and they replied, "We do not 'not like people who are not Jewish.' We just have our beliefs and values and want to share them with our children."

There was then a discussion about the family's values and beliefs. Rachel stood her ground by saying that her parents were alienating her as well as her friends by the way they talked about these beliefs. The parents came to understand Rachel's perspective. They said they wanted her to be able to make some choices, but that they couldn't agree with choices that went against their strongly held beliefs.

Her parents and Rachel agreed to disagree, and there was an understanding about what Rachel had been experiencing. The parents would not continue to say negative things to Rachel about her friends, because they finally understood.

Rachel chose to go to Israel the following summer and became more involved in Judaism as a result. Once she had their permission to make her own choices, she was able to stop rebelling and to begin to see things from her parents' point of view. Rachel made a different choice.

Rachel's older brother had been allergic to animals. They had never been able to have any pets. Now the two oldest had gone off to college and out to work. One was in medical school and one was working and living in another city. It was just Rachel at home. She said, "Now there is *no* reason why I can't have a cat, because there are no allergic people here."

The parents said, "Well, I guess that's probably true." She asked if I would support her in getting this cat. We talked about it a great deal in her therapy. I was trying to have her communicate in a different way with her parents. The way that she would previously *demand* things would always result in a fight. It had been impossible to have a normal conversation. We began to talk about negotiation.

In the course of the "cat discussion," the father said, "Okay. My secretary raises Persian cats. They are all pedigreed and we'll get you one of those."

Rachel said, "No. I want to go to the Animal Rescue League and get a cat."

Dad said, "No, no, no. You don't want a cat from the Animal Rescue League. You don't know anything about them. You don't know where they come from, or what they might be carrying."

I sat there watching as Rachel's face turned into the sky before a storm. She was furious. Her mother completely understood. She looked at me in panic and I said, "Well, what are you hearing right now?"

Mom said, "Well, I think that maybe Rachel's identifying with the cats from the Animal Rescue League, and maybe we are learning something about the way she feels." We talked about it. Dad eventually got it and he said, "You're right."

It was a most interesting conversation. Rachel was going to be able to go to the pound and get her little cat. The parents agreed to that. There are some very obvious things that are very "unobvious" in adoptive families. There are some ways that children make sense of some of the messages that are being given that are not at all what the parents *mean* to say.

Emily's story   Emily came to see me with her family at the age of about twelve or thirteen. They were concerned about her because she was shaving her head and wearing what they felt were "strange" clothes. Emily was creative and was acting out in very safe ways. She was expressing herself and trying to figure out who she was not in order to figure out who she was. Emily had been adopted as an infant.

Her older brother was also adopted and he had had a hard time making sense of who he was. I remember the first meeting and how much Emily did *not* want to be in my office. I asked her parents what the problem was and they looked at me like I must be either blind or insane! "Look!" they said. "It is so embarrassing when we go to church." I said, "Oh, isn't that wonderful that she goes to church with you." Now I knew they thought I was useless, but I had Emily's attention.

I asked if they were disappointed and embarrassed about how she looked and they said, "yes," and then I asked her if they were embarrassing to her and she said, *"yes."* They were at a typical juncture in adolescent development.

In adoptive families, the additional problem is that there are many ghosts in the room. There were the birth children that this family might have had, who, in their fantasy, would not look like this! And there were the birth parents, who in Emily's fantasy would have been "cool" and understanding.

Emily was an amazing person, as were her parents. They had stronger and stronger communication and learned to negotiate changes as she progressed from grade to grade. With all of her talents, Emily had the usual low self-esteem that adoptees have and she was reluctant to apply to very good colleges. Finally her parents, guidance counselor, and I must have made some dents.

The following is one of her college application essays.

Essay Topic: Evaluate a significant experience or achievement that has special meaning to you.

One of the best feelings about waking up just before dawn is being able to experience one of mother nature's magical creations: a sunrise. During this wondrous time, I am alert; there are no gray walls that block my mind from being at peace with myself and my thoughts . . . just hazy purples, pinks and azures that speckle the horizon.

My mind unfogs at 5:00 A.M., a time when I accomplish most of my thinking . . . not of the day's schedule running through my head, but questions about my inner self—who I am to myself, to others, and how I am a part of the scene that daylight reveals.

One morning on a gray, clouded dawn last October, I awoke to thoughts about my adoption and realized how isolated and lonely I felt because of being adopted: I am alone on a beach where waves spread across the sand and whisper to me. Bending down, I scoop a handful of salty seawater, splash my face, and try to free myself from this desolate island. Again, the ocean swirls around my feet and retreats.

Adoption means individuality for me. I have not found my roots yet, so I am free to be blown by the wind, to express myself. I am sensitive to everything and everything affects the way that I feel. Am I a blade of sea grass? Do the dunes need me? I have a feeling of nonexistence, a feeling of never being born and never having to die, but still I am as constant as the ocean and the changing of dawn into day.

I communicate with people as well as with nature, but with nature the connection is deeper and more personal, for I have adopted nature, taken her into my mornings. Always she comforts and soothes me. People were unable to soothe my alienation because they did not understand; I did not let them.

Three months have passed since that October morning and the sun shines brighter for me each day. Now I can see a sunrise without looking toward the sky because I have faith—the sun will rise without me. I have not abandoned nature, but I have let her absorb my feelings of isolation. I no longer feel marooned and lonely because of my adoption. I feel unified within myself and other people.

The dawn was gray this morning but I found beauty in the grayness, something special in it, for I have become whole. I have turned the gray into pearls from the ocean and now I toss them back onto the shore so that someone else who happens upon them may be as lucky as I.

Adolescence is complex. The world of adoption is complex. Without an understanding of this world by the professionals who are working with these families, the families and kids can be "pathologized," resulting in further disconnection when that is the last thing they need. It is the responsibility of the professionals who serve these families to learn about what is normal under the circumstances in the family created by adoption.

Chapter 5
The adopted adolescent and young adult

Adoption issues do not end at the threshold of adulthood—far from it. They continue throughout the life of the adopted person, and into the next generations, for all parties connected to adoption.

We have seen how children of adopted people and the children of birth parents often act out the story of the adoption, if it is not completed in the lifetime of their parents. (In the story of Sam and his late wife Rose, for instance, Sam's granddaughter was the one compelled to fulfill a search on the part of her mother.) I have learned, through over twenty-five years of adoption work, that when an adopted person does not choose to search—and many do not, which is a choice that should be respected—often the children of the adoptee exhibit the same behavior patterns and needs that we typically see in adopted people (more on these below) and many carry out a search for their birth grandparents.

The personal search for self for every person accelerates in late adolescence and early adulthood, which means, for an adopted person, that these are times of distinct "normative crisis." For an adopted person, typical events and stages of late adolescence and early adulthood —applying to college, moving away from home, beginning a family— carry with them many strong and serious issues. The presenting factors may not have anything to do with adoption per se, but with the experiences and emotions surrounding it. These are issues we don't label "adoption," but they do underlie adoption in a continuing and fundamental way.

Searching for a self that incorporates one's past and one's present is a normal life pursuit for all human beings. It takes on larger proportions when information is missing, obscured, or unknown. There is, in late adolescence and early adulthood especially, a need to find out where we came from in order to figure out where we are going. Yet the information many adoptees need about their past families, past cultures, past countries, is often not known. There is a need to know our ancestors in order to recognize our children. The search is something that all human beings do in one way or another. The second generation of an immigrant family finds a need to return to the "old country" and to give their children ethnic names. It is not disrespect for one's present family that leads one to search for the past. It is a human need to know as much as we can about who we are.

Both men and women who are adopted want to know, but women most often voice their desire to search earlier. It is in adolescence that most women begin to want to know more; for a number of men, their search begins at a rite of passage such as marriage or the birth of a child or death of a parent. The decision to search is a normal one, not a symptom of a problem: it is a normative crisis for the adopted person.

Because a search—either an actual search for a birth parent and origins or an internal search for adult identity—is such a basic theme for the adopted late adolescent and early adult, I give several stories about searching. Each one illustrates different challenges and responses to the urge to search.

Lucy's story   Lucy's adoptive family had four birth children, four adopted children, and a succession of foster children. Lucy had seen many children come into her family and was aware that some of their birth and foster parents were abusive and some were in drug rehabilitation programs or in jail. She knew quite a few of the scenarios in which a child could end up in foster care.

I first met Lucy when she was eighteen. She had applied to colleges, been accepted at several good schools, and had chosen to go to Princeton. It was her last spring at home before going away to college, and since she was constantly asking about her background, her parents felt they should tell her, while she was still at home, some disturbing facts about her birth family. Lucy's charts from the state agency had stated that both of her birth parents were retarded and that her birth mother had a particularly low IQ.

Lucy's parents told her what they knew and shortly afterward called me for an appointment to discuss the fallout. We all met in my office, and the first thing Lucy's mother said to me was, "We thought that telling Lucy was going to be so hard, but it wasn't!"

Lucy nodded and said, "You know, I fell off my bike when I was thirteen and hit my head. When I went to the pediatrician, he looked at the X-rays of my head and I heard him say there are early head injuries. I always figured I was abused or neglected as an infant, and that's how my parents ended up with me. I've seen a lot of other kids come into our house like that. So this wasn't a surprise to me."

I asked, "What about the retarded part?" Lucy shot back, "Well, I'm not retarded. I got into Princeton!" And a moment later, "My birth parents must not have been retarded." I said, "No, I don't think they were. I think that is a label that got put on your birth mother." What might have happened, as we reconstructed it with the adoptive parents, is that Lucy's birth mother had been severely abused by her own mother. She probably had suffered brain damage from head trauma over time. A social worker had realized she was slow but had misinterpreted it as actual retardation.

What was written in the chart was incorrect and misleading. But the information about her past, as we thought it through, was real, and it was important for Lucy to know it. Lucy's adoptive parents had taken her directly from the hospital, where she had been kept after birth due to symptoms of abuse.

⁜

There is an attitude that adopted people must be protected from difficult information about their birth family or about their early history. There is a feeling that somehow they are fragile and won't be able to handle the facts. Most of us, though, have skeletons in our closet: this is a part of any family history. And even when there is negative information, there can be positive results. In Lucy's case, the confirmation of what she already half-knew about her birth mother allowed her to have faith in her own intelligence, and to go off to college knowing who she was, and who she wasn't. I remember another story from the news about a young woman who discovered that her birth mother was a bag lady living in Central Park in New York. This was obviously a particularly difficult discovery, but, even so, the young woman felt it had helped her make sense of her history and her adoption. She could much more easily understand that her birth mother had hardly been able to take care of herself, so how could she have taken care of a child? The young woman could finally make sense of "why" she was given up for adoption. It is actually much harder for adopted people to learn that their birth parents are middle-class, were married at the time of the adoption, or have since married. The "nicer" stories make it harder to make sense of the decision.

Adopted people for the most part feel they don't exercise much control in their own lives. They were placed. Their names were changed. Everything's been done *to* them. I always say that being adopted is sort of like being in an F.B.I. witness protection program.

For young adults who choose to search for birth parents—and I do think that a search is something people have to *choose* to do themselves; it's much too big a process to be foisted on someone—it can be an important move away from the sense of impassivity that's colored their lives. The search and the information it yields can give one the experience of having control over one's life.

The experience of a young man who I'm working with now, though, shows that the timing of a search is crucial. The information is powerful and needs to be internalized at a pace that is organic. Eliot is now thirty-two. When he was twenty-one, he lived in the U.K., where he'd been adopted from. He did a search and met both of his birth parents and some siblings, and then he left his country. For eleven years his attitude had been, "Well, I completed my search and that's done." Because he ended up working with children with special needs, he began to see some of his own issues reflected back to him. Only now, in therapy, is he beginning to make sense of this. He's just beginning to make sense of his search and what he learned.

He's beginning to get angry about certain things he wasn't allowing himself to acknowledge, and to feel connected to certain things he wasn't allowing himself to feel connected to. People often think that because records are open in most other countries—as in the U.K. where Eliot was born—that people all search and assimilate the information they find much more quickly. Yet the search and the reunion are two very separate matters.

❖

An idea that many adopted people carry around is that at age eighteen they will no longer be adopted, that they will no longer belong to their adoptive family. Many of them were told as children that they could search for their birth family at eighteen or twenty-one, and they formed the idea then that this meant there'd be no "going home" afterward. No one ever *told* them this, but there is this idea, this feeling, for many of the adopted people that we work with. They, in reaction, often decide to stay home—often with a vengeance. Because where will they go? Leaving home to these young adults means that they won't have an identity.

We have had many parents come in to complain that their child, now in his or her mid-twenties, is burrowed into a room with every item he or she has ever owned packed in around them. Are they *ever* going to leave?

The most drastic therapy I ever did was to suggest that a family actually relocate in order to get their young adult adopted person out on her own. They found her an apartment, and they moved her carefully, caringly, and with much support. Then they moved themselves. This turned into a fine growth experience for the daughter, but it was also the only way that she ever would have left home. Obviously, this method would not be my suggestion in most situations!

At the other extreme, as we've seen in the previous chapter, are the kids who run away, or steal cars, or cause other serious trouble in order to make themselves unwanted and to provoke rejection. Adopted adolescents often do things to see if they will be rejected. Since they sometimes fear that in a sense they will no longer be adopted after they reach adulthood, they also want to be in control of the rejection by causing it rather than having it happen to them.

In many of these families, not only do the kids have problems about loss and ending, but so do the parents. Whether the parents have confronted their feelings about their infertility or not talked about it at all since the adoption is an important factor, strangely enough, in how separation plays out in the family. If an infertility issue is subconsciously being reworked by parents, the issues of loss for the adopted child, even though he or she is grown at this point, continue to be a challenge. Families need support and help with strategies for how to talk about feelings of loss. The family must learn to communicate, but also to separate, to form a new and stronger relationship with their adult child.

Transition to adulthood is hard enough for everyone. It is compounded by the identity confusion that adopted people experience. And adopted adolescents and young adults who were internationally or transracially adopted often have an especially difficult time. They are not only dealing with identity issues as adoptees ignorant of their genetic inheritance, but also struggling with racial identity and ethnic confusion.

Tiffany's story   Tiffany was biracial—half African American and half Caucasian. She had been adopted as an infant by a white family and had grown up happily in the suburbs in an extremely white environment. As a matter of fact, she says that she never actually saw a person of color until she was about thirteen. At a private high school dance in a nearby city, a black teenager asked her to dance. Tiffany said no and told her friends she thought he was a geek. In fact, she was confused and frightened by him. Tiffany had a difficult adolescence. No boys asked her out although she was quite a beautiful young woman.

Her parents were worried about her, and by the time Tiffany had turned fifteen, her mother had decided that she would benefit from contact with her birth mother. Tiffany's mother had figured out that the birth mother was a well-known TV anchor. She contacted the woman and went to meet her. Soon afterward, Tiffany met her birth mother, who is African American, and was introduced to a half-brother; it turned out he was the geek from the high school dance. Tiffany's birth mother had had him before she went to college. He was being raised by a grandmother and had come to live with his mother during his adolescence; he attended the boarding school where Tiffany had first met him. Tiffany came to see me, plopped down on my couch, and said, "Can you imagine?! What if I had gone out with him?"

Tiffany eventually met her extended birth family who lived in the South. She learned that her birth father was white and that he was now a prominent surgeon, married to a white woman and with three children. When she contacted him, he told her that he wanted to keep her a secret. He said that he had met her birth mother in college and had loved her but knew he could never marry her. The same racist issues from the past were definitely still alive for the birth father in the present. He'd felt he had to keep Tiffany's mother a secret fifteen years before, and he felt now that he had to keep Tiffany a secret. She was furious and very hurt.

Tiffany's own parents were nervous as her new relationships with her birth family formed, but they were supportive of her throughout all of this exploration.

Her birth mother moved to New York during Tiffany's late adolescence, and, when it came time for college, Tiffany decided on N.Y.U. She went off to school, hoping to get a good education and to be somewhat near her birth mother so they could develop a relationship.

Unfortunately, Loretta, her birth mother, had a busy schedule and hectic life and had little time for Tiffany. Tiffany felt isolated and alone at school, too. She called me one night, very distraught. She said she'd been asked to join a black sorority. I said I thought that sounded great. She burst into tears and said, "But I'm afraid of being with so many black people, and none of the white students befriend me. I'm neither black nor white—I am all alone."

Her next plan was to transfer to Spelman, where she would immerse herself in the life of this black women's college. She said, "I'd better learn to realize that the rest of the world sees me as black. I have to learn to be comfortable being black." Tiffany has spent a great deal of emotional energy in her late adolescence and early adulthood trying to make sense of her origins and identity. She has had to learn who she is inside herself, and who she is in both of her families, and who she is when the world looks only at her outer self. It is quite a feat, but one that many transracially adopted people must tackle.

Sylvia's poem   Sylvia is a young woman who was adopted as an older child from a Latin American country. She tells us in no uncertain terms in her poem how difficult it is to meld her past and her present:

See One Face

THIS IS DEDICATED TO THOSE WHO HAVE COME FROM DIFFERENT COUNTRIES, BEEN IN FOSTER HOMES, OR BEEN TAKEN CARE OF BY OTHER PEOPLE. FOR THOSE OF YOU WHO DON'T KNOW, I'M ADOPTED.

When I look into the mirror I see two faces.
When I look at my life, I lead two lives.
Like happy and sad.
Like hand and glove.
Like bitter tears and sweet laughter.
I have mastered my two lives.
I'm that girl who walks with poise, charisma, and class.
I make heads turn with the sway of my hips,

And my puckered-out luscious lips.
The hair on my head stands for the roots of my ancestors.
My radiant skin has been passed down to me from the greatest of
all Grandfathers,
And in my head I keep memories of my country,
Because that is all I have left.
And I daydream and stare into nowhere.
And I reminisce, reminisce, reminisce.
Then the horn beeps.
I am startled, not knowing where I am.
I think, could it be?
Did my daydream come true?
I'm hoping and wishing I'm in my village.
But then I realize I'm out in front of my school waiting for my new
life to pick me up.
And people no longer see my ancestors.
They only see confusion.
And when I come home to my new life,
I live in the lap of luxury.
I eat like a queen.
I have a hard time deciding what to wear in the morning because
I have so much.
I'm not trying to brag, but I would give it all up
If I could only have the same last name,
The same Mother and Father,
The same home, and the same country.
So when I look in the mirror I only want to see one face,
And when I lead my life, I only want to lead one life.

Silvia Noelia Ramos
(Silvia Elizabeth Leary)
June 1997

Vanessa's letter   Vanessa was the third child adopted into a family with four adopted children that lived in my city. The parents were white, the oldest child was Latino, the middle child was African American, Vanessa was adopted from Korea at age two, and her younger brother was adopted from Vietnam. Vanessa grew, and over the years I saw her with her family and with her friends. Vanessa began to wonder about her past life, in a serious way, when she was in high school, and she began to see me off and on in therapy. She decided to spend her summer before college in Europe with friends, and I received many letters and cards from her then. Here is an excerpt from one:

> *I have been having a lot of fun, but I'm homesick. The funny thing is that I don't know if I'm homesick for Cambridge or for Korea. I feel as if I don't know why I am in Europe. My friends are all talking about their ancestors and that this is where they came from. What am I doing? I went to an expo in Seville. I went to the Korean shops there and I asked one woman where she was from and she said Seoul and we started chatting. I was born in Seoul. She asked if I had ever been back (she must have known I was adopted or that I wasn't "quite" Korean). I asked if she knew Korean and how to write in Korean and she said yes. I asked if she could write my Korean name, Park Kim Mee, and she wrote it on a bag I was carrying. My eyes started to water as I saw her writing it down and I just couldn't stop. (You know I don't like to cry in front of people.) My name in Korean looked so pretty. I realized I had never seen my name before in Korean characters. I don't even know how to pronounce it properly. The woman had to correct me. I thanked her very much, but I could not look her in the eye. That woman has made me feel that I need to go to Korea and that I need to go soon. I do want to learn some Korean, though, before I go.*

Vanessa signed in her Korean characters. Her letter conveys the terrible homesickness that many adopted people feel in their adolescence as they try to figure out where they came from in order to figure out where they will go as adults.

Sometimes internationally and transracially adopted people feel that same-race adopted people don't understand this homesickness for fixed identity. And yet, I believe all adopted people experience a similar yearning and confusion. These are just feelings that are complicated further by moving between different races, religions, ethnicities, cultures.

Another poem, by Penny Callan Partridge, speaks to this sameness and difference among adopted people:

Responding to a Poem by Mi Ok Bruining

This Korean-born adoptee
is translating herself
back into Korean so she can
greet her omoni and
even if only in fantasy
feel she is getting across.

This Korean-born adoptee
will funnel herself
down through these
words she has learned to say
back into the arms she has
learned to imagine.

This Korean-born adoptee
once hated this white bread
California-born adoptee's
using bicultural
experience
as metaphor.

But Mi Ok, even though
I had no ocean or border
or linguistic barrier to
get across, I was
still trying to figure out
how I was translated.

If I grant you many differences,
will you grant me this one
sameness? That we are not
as much from either side
as we are those who translate
are those who are translated.

The move from childhood to adulthood is a particularly complex one. The adopted person considering starting a family is burdened by societal messages about birth parents, about legitimacy, about infertility, and about choice.

It was not until the birth of her first child that Katrina, an adult adopted person, suspected the intensity of her feelings of abandonment and her own fiercely protective maternal feelings.

Katrina had been adopted as an infant by an abusive family and her life growing up was dismal. Being adopted is very hard to make sense of, but being adopted and then terribly abused by adoptive parents is even harder to come to terms with. Katrina ran off as soon as she was in her late adolescence and got married. Her adoptive parents were Jewish, so she married a young man whose father was a Protestant minister. When Katrina was in her early twenties, she decided, with support from her husband and his family, to search for her birth family. She found her birth parents. They were married to each other and had two sons . . . full siblings. Katrina's mother, Lane, told her the story.

Lane had been in college when she met Katrina's father, Warren. They were in love, and before long Lane realized she was pregnant. She told her parents, who were distraught. Lane's parents were white Anglo-Saxon Protestants and well to do. Warren's parents were also upper middle class, but Jewish. The two sets of parents talked and decided for the "kids" that the best plan would be to give the baby up for adoption. Lane was sent off to live with an aunt, and her friends were told that she was living abroad. The baby was born and placed for adoption. Lane's sadness never left her. Two years later, when Warren was in law school, they decided to marry anyway. They have lived together all of these years and have held the memory of the baby that they lost.

They were shocked and thrilled at the same time when Katrina appeared. I spent some time with all of them as they tried to figure out what was appropriate. Katrina divorced her first husband. She had been very young when they married. She went back to school, now that she had permission and genes to be smart. She married a young man who was Jewish. She moved closer to her birth family.

Soon Katrina and her husband Sam were awaiting their first child. In her journal she wrote this amazing account of leaving the hospital with her baby, Sara.

On November 14, 1992, at 12:05 P.M., my mother, from whom I was separated for twenty-one years, held her first grandchild, my daughter. Sara, my joy, and my connection to this world, was only twenty minutes old. I cried, but not even for thirty seconds, and that could have been from exhaustion or relief. Two days later, my husband and I were given discharge instructions. We collected the things in our room, dressed our precious tiny bundle, and put her in the hospital-provided cart. Walking past the nurses' station, I felt as if something were slowing me down. I started to feel—sad, I suppose. I felt I wanted to say good-bye to the nurses who had been more than kind and nurturing. I wanted to thank them for sharing the most intimate event of my life. But the shift had changed, and I didn't see any of the nurses who had been there for me, for us. I forced a smile as we walked past the station and around the corner to the nursery.

This was my first visit to the nursery. Sara had stayed with me in my room except for a brief visit to the nursery with her father when she was first born. I looked around at all of the babies tightly wrapped, alone in separate carts, the carts pushed into a huddle under the bright fluorescent lights. The two nursery nurses were busy discharging patients. What if one of the babies cried? I thought. What if one of them needed someone but wasn't crying?

So that I wouldn't cry, I looked away and gazed at my daughter, occasionally glancing at my husband as we waited our turn. "Most parents wait outside for this" (the testing, temperature taking, shots) we were told. "No, that's okay, we'd like to stay," I said, perfectly calm, casual, and reasonable. To myself, I thought, It's this way or no way at all! The fierceness of feeling accompanying that private thought surprised me. I wondered what my facial expression was, so I checked in a mirror. Good. I looked fine. A little tired, maybe, but okay.

I heard one nurse say to the other, "Better call the doctor, he may want her to stay." What? "What?" I said, holding onto Sara's cart and grabbing Sam's arm. "Oh," said the nurse, "her temperature is a little high. Here, give her some of this water and maybe that will help." I could feel myself fighting back tears but I had to stay in control; I had to help Sara and get us out of here! "Did you hear that?" I said to my husband, who was starting to look worried—frightened really—or was that my projection? "She's going to be fine. Let's give her the water," he said.

Like an angel, like the "team player" we needed, Sara drank every last drop. This took some time, and silently I made a plan.

If the nurse came back and said, "We've talked to the pediatrician and he would like her to stay," I would respond by saying, "Okay, I'll stay as well." If that wasn't allowed, I had plan B. I would pick up Sara and wielding . . . what? My hand? A baby bottle? I would say quietly and calmly, "Stay back, we're leaving. Don't try to stop us and no one will get hurt." *We can do it, I thought; two of "us," two of "them."* "What if they call security?" *I thought. The nurse broke into my daydream to say,* "No problem. Sara can go home. Take these bottles with you, just make sure she drinks them." "Thank you," *I said. My husband smiled and touched my arm and I started to cry big drops of silent tears. I did not want Sara to see me cry, but now the tears were streaming, still silently.* "It's okay," *said the nurse,* "happens all the time. If you hadn't cried I would have thought your hormones had dried up!" *Alright, I'm okay now.* Why had I made her into an enemy?

I picked up Sara, covered in a blanket, out of her cart and we walked to the elevator. A nurse was standing by the control panel, and to one side was the woman who hosted the newborn channel. I recognized her but didn't want to take my eyes off of Sara to speak to her. Next, two loud men got on the elevator. We're leaving the hospital and going home with our baby daughter. *She had been born two and a half weeks early and I didn't think we'd be ready. Grinning now, breathing slowly and deeply, I moved to get off the elevator. So did the two men—and the nurse by the control panel said,* "Wait for the baby, please!" *That was us. That's okay, this is the world—there are rude people and there are people like the nurse.*

My husband went out to get the car while I waited by the glass doors. An older woman walked by and said, "I don't think she's dressed warmly enough." "It's all right," *I said.* "She's going right into a heated car." What? *Was that me speaking? I don't know if she's dressed warmly enough!* I should have just ignored her. Oh, here's Sam. Oh, it is cold out. Poor baby. "Here, take her," *I said and insisted on waiting outside the car so that Sam could put her into her car seat, with the heat running and the doors closed. I could see Sam shaking his head as I was shivering in the cold. I didn't feel anything except caring what Sara feels. I got into the back seat with the baby, and my husband started to drive off, and, in that very moment, without hesitation or space for a thought, I began sobbing, shrieking, moaning. "Her head, her head—she's too little—something is going to happen to her—this car seat is too big, it's too big—her neck will break—SLOW DOWN!" At first Sam tried to respond to my fears by saying, "It's okay. She's fine. We'll be home soon." Then he slowed down to a crawl as I continued to sob. Even looking at Sara and knowing that I did not want to have my daughter see my tears did not change things. Finally we were home.* Sara is all right. *Sam, keeping his sense of humor, said he had considered dropping me off at the local psychiatric hospital. He went out that day and bought a smaller infant-sized car seat.*

Three months later, although I found that there could have been several "reasons" for my reaction, I can see that they all come under the idea, the act, of leaving the hospital with my daughter. For as long as I can remember, for me, the point of no return was not when my birth father refused to marry my mother (he changed his mind three years later). It was not when my mother and grandparents met with the social worker at the Children's Home Society. It was not even when my mother signed "papers." It was when my mother actually left the hospital. *I was left in the care of what? Two nurses? Where? In a cart under bright lights. Certainly I was not in the care of two people so very protective, so fiercely loving of me that they (intelligent, reasonable, easygoing) would be ready to kill or die without hesitation to protect me. My husband and I became these two people the moment we knew Sara would be joining us in nine months. We were both pro-choice, with a decent understanding of biology, but nothing could have stopped us from mothering and fathering for those nine months. And then, finally, to have the object of our love, our daughter, in our arms, was overwhelming.*

Perhaps I was sobbing because my heart was breaking and rebuilding at the very same time. Maybe that is the sound of a broken but enlarging heart. Breaking for myself, because I was left and because something did happen to that tiny baby in this big and sometimes cruel world: after three months in foster care, I was adopted by a couple who were very unlike my birth parents, and, I would learn later, were abusive. My heart was breaking for my mother because she did have to leave the hospital, and to do that, as a mother, I now know that a part of her died. I was weeping for that part of her that I'll never know, that she'll never know. When I say "part" I don't mean arm or leg or ear—Sara is a part of all of me—and so to leave her would be as if leaving a part of all of myself. I was crying because I knew just how unnatural an act she'd been forced to perform, because I know how her arms ached to hold her newborn daughter.

And weeping tears of joy for my daughter because she has her grandmother, because she has her mother. . . . As I'm writing this, I wonder about the power of what we bring—even preverbally—into adulthood and how far that follows us in what ways. Although there have been many times in my life when the "facts" of my life have seemed only sad, I now find with Sara that there is a feeling of wonderful strength, a feeling that actually began as I drove away from that hospital, as I was living an experience that I know the adults in my infant life were unable to live.

I wonder how much of this is about being a mother and how much is about being a parent. I wonder what it will all mean to Sara. I wonder how all of this will change and will mean something else over time. Will the feelings diminish, or be reworked as she lives for the first precious time in a family that is both related and together? What will it all mean when, and if, I enter "grandmotherhood?"

Just, but not simply, what will it mean.

⁜

I began this chapter by saying that adoption issues continue throughout the life of an adopted person. One day last summer, as I sat at my computer, in the midst of writing this book, and glancing now and then out at the dunes, the sea grass, and the mesmerizing colors of the sky in Truro on Cape Cod, I was given the chance to think how this had been so for me and for my adopted friends and colleagues. The telephone rang that morning, and it was a magazine editor asking me to answer some questions about how adult adopted people feel, about how their lives are affected by the deeper or core issues of adoption. I carefully answered her questions, hung up the telephone, and then remembered vividly an evening almost ten years ago when I was sitting around with four of my best friends, all of whom are adopted. I remembered a long, hilarious session making fun of ourselves and our adoptee neuroses. I will share a bit of what we talked about.

We adopted people were *taken*, and *moved*, and *transplanted*, and given *new* names and *new* identities. We all have some trauma related to this early (or not so early, in some cases) event.

We carry around some trauma associated with our first loss and with any additional moves and losses.

But the thing that comes along with these losses is our adaptive qualities. We can get along anywhere as a result of our early experience with transplanting and replanting. Place us in a room with high society, we're fine. Our birth parents may have been kings and queens, after all. Place us in a room with junkies and low-life thieves, we'll be hanging out and talking trash with them in no time. Our birth parents could have been the lowest of the low. Place us in challenging schools and we'll either do just fine (aiming to please), or we'll be so busy trying to get the social thing down (we *have* to be accepted, after all) that we'll forget our assignments and do poorly academically. But we'll be working on something: We just adapt and adapt. We're actors trying on many roles, because we could be anyone, couldn't we? We started out as one person, after all, and then turned into another. We know how to act and how to get along just fine, anywhere and with anyone, thank you.

Many of us were told that our birth parents were poor and unable to parent, so we gravitate toward a lower socioeconomic group of friends at certain periods, or we work with this population in order to give something back to "our people." We take what you say *very* seriously. If you put down what we know or imagine is our background in any way, it only adds to our loss of self-esteem. When you express love and respect for our culture, for our race, for our religion, our ethnicity of root family, as well as for what we've gained from our family by adoption, we hear you.

Intimacy? It takes knowing who you are to know who you can be with another. So, we either get dependent and mushy and enmeshed and then feel rejected, or we do the opposite and stay in our marginal unattached stance. After all, we fit in two families (or more) while, at the same time, we fit in neither of these families completely. We are excellent bystanders: we can see things from any angle. We make great therapists, great detectives, great friends and family members (although we can be hard to live with as we sort out our divided loyalties and losses). When we decide to be loyal, we are *eternally* loyal, like a beagle.

Attachment? We were uprooted; our roots are delicate because they've once (maybe twice or more) been torn. We will reattach well once, if the people we're placed with are also good at attaching (it takes two). But don't move us too often, or we'll have no ability to stick to it. We'll get too good at moving from place to place and will have a hard time with jobs and with relationships. We learn well and early: too often we've been taught about attachment by being taken away, and then placed, and then taken away. So we attach on the surface very quickly; it's part of how we adapt. We can't even walk into a hotel room for an overnight stay without rearranging furniture so we can settle. We need to bring along a transitional object—a familiar object—when we're in strange places. After all, our first familiar object, our birth mother, disappeared!

Loss? Loss is a pervasive issue. We deal with it in many different ways. Some of us are pack rats and keep everything—every shred of everything. We collect old things, "useless" things, because this is what society has often thought of us. We have to have one of every color of our favorite sweater: What if we lose one? Our rooms are cluttered and piled high with things that we can't lose, because we're trying to calm our feelings about the people that we've lost. Some of us go to the other extreme and keep nothing. We give things away. We'd rather be in control and know where things are, even if they're with someone else. We live sparsely and can't bear to have anything that might end up being lost. It is the same issue; it just manifests itself differently for some of us than others. People misdiagnose some of us as having attention deficit disorder but, actually, we all have a problem with distraction because it feels like . . . *something is missing.*

Anger? How would you feel if people had done things to you when you were an infant or small child, when you were essentially unconscious? Your whole world was destabilized, and then, like magic, you were a different person. It's okay. We can deal, but there's going to be some anger. No longer toward our parents, birth or adoptive—they had their own problems and losses to contend with as we all did—but at the situation. We older adopted people, whose adoption took place in the especially closed era, can't stand secrecy and get very angry if people are clandestine or hide things through passive aggression. Just tell us the truth! The truth may hurt, but having it kept from us is even more devastating and infuriating. The truth is what we've always wanted. Openness and sincerity. Our anger is dynamic. It moves us to get involved politically, to want to change the world because our world was changed so dramatically. We can focus our anger and use it to challenge what is wrong. We can be agents of change, as we were infants and children of change. Change is our legacy and our strength as well as our downfall.

Humor? Humor is the highest defense mechanism. We were quick to learn whatever we needed to in order to survive. We learned this from our birth parents, and we learned this from our adoptive parents. We can laugh at ourselves (but don't you laugh at us). We can laugh at the world around us. We have the gift of play and fantasy because we have lived in a world of fantasy and of not-knowing for all of our lives.

Spirit? We have an innate sense of spirit and spirituality. It doesn't matter what religion our birth parents had, or what religion our adoptive parents practiced. It is not about organized religion or disorganized religion. It is about something much deeper and more personal. It is about the archetypal themes in our lives as adoptees. We spend our lifetimes delving into who we are, and where we come from, and where we are going. We wonder why we are here and what we will leave behind— in the name of all of our fathers and all of our mothers.

Chapter 6
Keeping connections

In the early twentieth century there was a movement away from collective care of dependent children in orphanages and foundling hospitals to more individual care in foster and adoptive homes. Children had a better chance of survival in family homes, and they were given to parents by grateful authorities with minimal investigation. It was during this period, around the late 1930s, that the "chosen child" became a reality. Prospective parents could walk down the rows of cribs and choose the child who appealed to them most, or agencies would select a child and arrange a meeting for the parents and child in their offices. Children were considered lucky to be chosen, and little attention was given to the separation and adjustment problems that resulted. The institution retained custody of the foundling so that if the covenant were breached or the parents died, leaving no provisions for the children, the agency could resume care, taking the child back into the institution. Because of this temporary feeling, there was not always full commitment to adoption.

The courts and agencies became involved in adoption in the 1930s, with the legalization of adoption. The movement to close records, referred to by some as the "Nosy Neighbor Act," occurred at the same time. The clear focus was upon the adopted person, who, child welfare workers argued, should not be held responsible for the "sins" of the birth parents. The adopted child was "reborn" as the child of the new family, with a new identity and a new identification in the form of a birth certificate, executed exactly as if the adoptee had been born to the adoptive parents. The original birth certificate was sealed and replaced with the new one, replete with lies—a legal fiction.

It has been assumed that the original reason for sealing the records was to protect the adopted person and adoptive parents from the intrusion of the birth parents and, in turn, to allow the birth parents to make a new life for themselves, free of responsibility for the child and safe from the disgrace resulting from errors of the past.

Sealing the records was actually a means of protecting the adoptive family from the intrusion of others. The motive, according to older social workers from that era, was to prevent reporters nosing around for news from coming upon something really juicy and publishing it, causing untold suffering and permanent damage. Unscrupulous relatives might trace a child if they wished, and use their knowledge to upset a well-established relationship, if they did not do worse, or they might use it for blackmail.

Whatever the original reasons, the sealed records and total anonymity of the birth parents assumed enormous importance as the primary safeguard for adoptive families.

In the 1950s, after the Korean War, the first large number of international adoptions took place. These were done predominantly through church organizations. The 1958 Adoption Act is the basis of our current legislation, and, though the world has changed dramatically, our practice of adoption has not changed in many ways.

A 1950s monograph by John Bowlby demonstrated the deleterious effects on the child of early maternal deprivation and was instrumental in bringing into adoption policy the current mental health theories, with an emphasis on early placement. It also caused a shift from the interest in heredity and genetic determinism to environmental and psychodynamic concerns. Much of the effort previously devoted to evaluating infants considered for adoption was then more properly devoted to a study of the "applicants" or preadoptive parents. Instead of searching for the perfect baby for a childless couple, the workers began to concern themselves with finding a good home for the child. The motto changed at that point from "a home for every child" to "the right parents for every child."

In the 1960s there was increasing awareness of the effects of loss and separation on the child. The peak year for documented adoptions by strangers was 1968, and 66 percent of these were babies under one year of age. Agencies began to concern themselves with family dynamic theory and to study the dynamic interplay between the adopted person and other family members.

Matching physical features and racial backgrounds was also a big concern, since it was felt that differences in appearance could severely hamper a child's capacity to identify with his or her adoptive parents. Every effort was made to match religious backgrounds and to find adoptive parents with similar temperaments and talents to those the child was assumed to have inherited.

In the 1970s there was a decline in the number of infants available for adoption because of efficient contraception, liberalized abortion laws, and support for single mothers. This was the beginning of the placement of older children and special needs children, and the increase in international adoptions and transracial adoptions.

This was also the beginning of the "permanency movement" in child welfare. There was more consciousness of the needs of the child. It was felt that it was better for the child to have continuity and to allow the adults to grieve if there were problems. "Legal risk" adoptions began being done rather than having children wait in foster homes before being placed in a permanent home. Less disruption was clearly better for the child, even if it was more difficult for all of the adults involved.

In 1975, the Children's Act was the first consideration of issues "in the best interest of the child." Adopted people gained the right to have access to their birth records (although this is still not upheld in most states); adoption allowances for families adopting special needs children were allotted; and the prohibition of private placements without the involvement of child welfare agencies to protect the children's rights and to counsel the birth and adoptive parents was endorsed.

In the 1980s, there was a growth in the placement of older children with special needs. Transracial adoptions continued to increase, and, with them, an awareness of the needs and difficulties for children adopted transracially. There were sweeping improvements in fertility counseling and in new reproductive technologies, which raised expectations for people struggling with infertility. A huge growth in intercountry adoptions came about in this decade from countries in Latin America, Central America, and Asia in particular.

The 1989 Children's Act emphasized an awareness of the birth parents' involvement and the value of a connection between birth and adoptive parents for the child. There was a recognition of the importance of the contract in adoption.

In the 1990s there has been greater recognition of the wide range of children's needs and families' needs in the more complex situations that our adoptions present, including infant, older child, transracial, international, special needs, foster adoptions, and guardianship.

Curiously, at this time of heightened awareness among child welfare professionals and compassionate adoption professionals, there has been a decline in adoptions arranged by child welfare agencies and a resurgence of the 1920s brand of private adoptions arranged by doctors, lawyers, and private practitioners, some of whom do not truly have the child's and families' best interests at heart. Some of this may be the unfortunate burgeoning of the business of adoption; some may be that birth and adoptive parents are taking matters into their own hands and creating more open arrangements without as much government intervention; some of it may be that the older child welfare agencies are not providing the current services that these families, birth and adoptive, need and want, so they turn elsewhere. Some of the professionals see adoption as a legal affair only, and enjoy the business of adoption without any awareness of the lifelong issues that all of the people whose lives are affected will face. Some agencies, doctors (in some countries), and lawyers who arrange private adoptions receive very high fees. Adopters willingly pay because they so dearly want a family. (In New Zealand no money is exchanged in an adoption, and all adoptions are handled by child welfare professionals.)

Illegal black market adoptions of children who have basically been stolen still occur. In gray market adoptions, both sets of parents may be deceived and misguided, but the actual adoption is done legally, though brokers attempt to get around the law and to place babies with the highest bidder. Independent adoptions can be either gray market or totally legal and ethical depending on the professionals who are doing them. Independent adoptions have become the predominant means of adoption in many parts of this country.

All adoptive parents must prepare to be investigated by the authorized agency before the adoption becomes final. In agency adoptions, this is done before taking the child. In gray and black market adoptions, the review is done at least six months after the child is in the adoptive home. In independent adoptions, in some states, the court, upon receiving the petition for adoption, requests that an investigation be made by the local child welfare department to assess the suitability of the adopting family, with the option of removing the child. This means, once again, the possibility of disruption and change for the child in the interest of the parents. This is a rather general description of what happens in these cases: there are no clear federal rules, and policy and laws vary from state to state.

The question in gray and black market adoptions becomes not, is this the best home for this child, but will this child suffer harm with these parents. This is no way to make decisions for children's lives or for the families, both birth and adoptive.

❖

It used to both amuse and infuriate me in the early 1980s when older children were being adopted in the public welfare system. At the adoption day in court, the records would be closed up and sealed. Birth certificates were changed, original birth certificates impounded.

These older children would, supposedly, become new people and would never have anything to do with their birth families again. They would have been subject to a "termination visit," which was seen as a painful but necessary procedure to allow the child and his birth mother, father, grandparents, or sibling to go on with their lives by participating in a clear "terminal" farewell. The same child, although his adoption was closed by the court, would go out to the telephone booth and call his grandmother the day after the adoption was finalized. The same grandmother he had called every week all of the other years before being adopted. The same grandmother he had visited while he was in foster care.

The adoptive parents would get angry when they were told by the social worker that this was illegal, or that this connection was not going to help the child to bond to the new family. There was no true understanding of the need that these children had for connection to the people who had been positive and present in their very complicated, and often traumatic, lives.

I believe there is no such thing as "termination" in the relationship between children and their birth families. Even if the birth parents die, it's not "over." By creating a ritual based on the pretense that the relationship has ended, the child's internal reality is at odds with the external one.

Most of the children we see clinically, especially those who are older at the time of their placement (both domestic and international) are emotionally preoccupied with these dissonances. They may not have words to describe the depth of their confusion or longing or rage, since these experiences most often occurred precognitively and pre-verbally.

They also may not have access to a neutral enough place to express thoughts and feelings that could be hard for their present family to understand or to acknowledge. These adopted children often come up with answers to their questions that are filled with fantasy, because there are no mirrors or receptors to help them make sense of their experience.

Having been detached from birth parents, birth family, birth community, and sometimes birth culture or race, children are not able to have that love or identity as part of their growing sense of self. It is difficult for the child to feel self-love when wondering, "Why didn't my first parents keep me?" if there is no ongoing experience of the birth parents' positive feelings.

It is our job to protect our children, and the children we work with, from harm. Child professionals are mandated to protect them from danger and abuse. We are not, however, mandated to protect them from the truth. The greatest gift that one can give children is to tell them their truths and to help them make sense of these truths, especially when they are complicated and harsh.

Our PACT team had an interesting opportunity several years ago. We did a twelve-session consultation with a private agency in the Boston area. The director of this agency was someone whom I'd known for many years, and because she trusted my work she allowed me to do some unusual things in the course of the work with this case.

PACT works as a team, often from behind a one-way mirror. One therapist is assigned to the family and is in the room with them. In this case, however, the "client" was the agency.

The agency wanted to improve their placement practice. Too many of their adoptions were failing, or disrupting, some just before the finalization, especially when attempting to place sibling sets together.

The agency thought that perhaps we could look at some cases and give them some idea how to change their approach to placement. They had one particular case in mind as a pilot.

There were two children, an eight-year-old girl and her four-year-old brother, who had been in a foster home for many years. The youngest had been placed there directly from the hospital. Their birth mother had signed the termination of parental rights long ago. The birth mother was a drug addict and had never been in treatment. She had not raised either of the children for very long. They had been with relatives, friends, and foster parents for all of their lives.

Since they were freed for adoption, they needed a permanent plan. They had been placed in two different homes already, and both placements had disrupted. The agency was about to place these children now for the third, and, they hoped, final time for adoption. They could not envision another disruption for these kids.

The little girl was sexually abused by one of her mother's boyfriends. The four-year-old was physically abused. The eight-year-old is white. Her four-year-old brother, who is her half-sibling, is biracial. These kids were placed in their foster home when the four-year-old was an infant. The foster parents are wonderful and very experienced. They had been parenting the kids for four years. They were not in a position to adopt the children and didn't plan to. They were in their sixties. Their birth and adopted children were all grown up. There was, however, a little kink. They had recently adopted another eight-year-old. This was making it very confusing for these children, who really liked where they were and wanted to stay.

The reason they had adopted the other eight-year-old was that he was terminally ill. They wanted to make sure that his placement was secure, so he could live his life with them. They could commit themselves to his very short life, but they felt that, in their sixties, they couldn't commit themselves to an eight-year-old and a four-year-old. So, for very good reasons, they were quite clear that they should not adopt these children, whom they loved.

The social workers involved in this case had been involved in it from the beginning. One of the social workers had known the children longer than anyone else and had been the only consistent person for them. She took the children every summer, for two weeks, to Maine to her summer home with her family to give the foster mother a respite.

These workers were very enmeshed with this family. There was the possibility of the kids sabotaging any placement plan because it would cut them off from the workers and from the foster parents, whom they loved, and who were the only adults they had ever trusted.

There was a possibility that any and all of these people could be sabotaging it directly or indirectly. We looked at the situation very carefully and thought about all of this information, and we immediately said that the only way that these kids could *ever* be adopted would be if it were an open adoption. The people who would adopt *must* be willing to keep the foster parents as "grandparents." They must be willing to allow the social worker to stay on as an "auntie," to keep an open relationship.

If you know that children have certain people in their lives who are their connection and their lifeline or attachment, then it is essential to keep those attachments intact for them. Repeated emotional disconnection is devastating and irreparable.

If we know this in advance, then we must look for a family that can not only tolerate but understand why the connection is important for these children. That family must be willing to include these people in their lives for the sake of the children.

We asked the agency to get some files out on their prospective adoptive parents—parents who would be able to be open in this kind of situation. They brought several files, and we went through them and talked about which families might work.

One particular family looked promising for many reasons. The mother had been previously married. She was white and had had two children with her former husband who was African American. Her oldest son was in the Air Force, and her daughter was a senior in high school. They had a good relationship with both their father and their mother.

Mother had remarried. She and her present husband (who was white) had a nine-year-old son. Her second husband had been very accepting of her children by the previous marriage, and he had a good rapport with their father—her exhusband.

It was a big and functional stepfamily / extended family situation. They had taken a high-risk adoption placement of a little girl who had been sexually abused. They had her with them for almost a year, at which time the birth mother was ready and able to take the child back. The perpetrator was no longer in the picture. The birth mother had had a lot of therapy, so family preservation was the correct route and the adoption did not go through. The child went back to her birth mother.

They were very saddened by this because they had really gotten to be close to her, and yet they were happy that her mother had been able to get her life together in a fairly short period of time. They still wanted to expand their family through adoption.

This family seemed to be worth exploring. One, they had experience with biracial issues. Two, they had experience with a sexually abused child. And, three, they were open and had stepfamily situations that they had handled quite well. We thought that we had better take a closer look.

We saw the family and talked to them at length, and then we suggested to the agency that the foster parents and the preadoptive parents go out for a breakfast and get to know each other. The social worker said, "Oh. Let me get my appointment book and I'll see. I could probably do that on Sunday the . . ." And I said, "No, no, no. You don't understand. What we're recommending is that the two sets of parents go out and have breakfast. Alone." She said, "Well, that's highly irregular. We don't usually do that. We actually never send adoptive parents—we couldn't possibly do that." And I said, "Well, I think perhaps you could try to do it. Because, if these people are going to have an open relationship, they are going to have to authentically like each other. Their relationship is not going to be based on any social worker's interventions. It's going to be based on their liking each other. I'd like to do this little experiment, to see if they can work things out and to see if they like each other."

She did not like it at all, but luckily, as I said, the director was a colleague who said, "It's okay. I am willing to take a risk and to see what happens. We can't afford for these kids to have another failed adoption." We sent these two couples out for breakfast and it was terrific. It was really an important event.

What was most important was that the foster father approved of the preadoptive father. This was a big concern, because he was extremely concerned about the little girl's sexual precocity. She is a challenge, as are most children who have been severely sexually abused and traumatized.

The boundaries were very important. The foster father had a lot of experience with this, and he really wanted to be sure that the adoptive father would be okay. At the end of the breakfast, the foster father approved of him. They also liked each other and they had things in common. This particular foster mother was a font of knowledge. She had worked out a very structured homework environment and had arranged an education plan and follow-through for the eight-year-old, who had attention deficit disorder and was involved in all kinds of therapy. The foster mother would be such a resource to any parent adopting this child.

Now that the foster family had approved of this preadoptive family, I wanted to meet the kids from the preadoptive family. They came in for a session with their family, except for the son who was in the Air Force, who couldn't come home at that time. In the course of that session we made a recommendation that the daughter and the younger son go and spend an overnight at the foster family's house. And the social worker said, "Wait a minute, now. You want us to bring the two little kids over to the preadoptive family?" She was always thinking that she wasn't quite understanding what I was saying and that she had to fix it somehow. And I said, "No. I'm suggesting that the preadoptive family kids spend an overnight at the foster family house." And she said, "Why that's highly irregular! We never do that." And I said, "Well, I know, but I think it's a good idea, because these little kids have been in at least three other homes and it's very scary when you go to a different home. I think it would be good for these bigger kids to know what that might feel like. This is going to be an open adoption, so these folks are going to be the grandparents. They have to get to know these people because they will be a part of their own extended family." Though the kids were reluctant at first, they ended up genuinely liking this family and getting to see their new adoptive siblings on their own turf and to understand them in a different way.

Eventually, after all of these unconventional interventions, the preadoptive family did take the kids. The agency kept wanting to push it—faster—once they had a family. And I kept saying, "No. One of the problems is this is too fast. There have to be transitions for these kids and it has to be done very carefully if you want it to work. They have to finish the school year at the school they're in, then slowly over the summer we'll do this move. Children have to have normal transitions." The way that foster and preadoptive kids get pulled out of one school and one home on a Tuesday afternoon and end up in another home and another school on Wednesday morning is not a good approach. How could anyone think it is? So we worked on that, and we talked about it. The placement was a good one, though not without problems! The primary therapist got a call in the middle of the night from the adoptive mother, who said, "Uhh—the eight-year-old is under the sheets with the eleven-year-old playing cards. What am I going to do?" And the therapist said, "Well, maybe you should go in and tell them it's a good idea to play cards in the living room. We should talk about it at the next session." So there were definitely problems. But the family had lots of resources. They could call the foster mother. They could call us. They could really work with it. And this is another of these brief long-term therapy cases, which means that we've kept in touch with the family and we see that it's going along really well.

Connections to the foster parents and to the social worker were a reasonable and clearly necessary part of the attachment process for these children. Those were connections that were very valuable and ended up being assets to the adoptive family.

As we began to see in the previous chapter, connections can be made, even in the most difficult and painful cases. The reality, the truth, is what is most important, because all adopted people think the worst if they have no facts.

Patricia's story The Hamiltons adopted Patricia at ten months from the Department of Social Services. They had an older birth child as well. The Hamiltons had been successful and good parents to David, and when they found that there was secondary infertility, they had decided to adopt. They knew that there were children waiting in the public system and chose that over a private adoption.

Patricia, who had always been a challenge, was hyperactive and had some learning problems. She was a searcher and had been trying to find out who she was and where she came from from the age of two. Patricia constantly asked about her birth family. After years of trying everything they could—and they were the best parents Patricia could have hoped for—the Hamiltons felt that the one thing they had not yet done for their daughter was to help her with a search. They had originally wanted to wait until she was twenty-one, but changed their minds after hearing me speak at a conference; I had brought up the concern that most young people who are eighteen to twenty-one—which is when most people think a person should have the right to search—are rather alone in the world . . . sort of dangling participles. I recommend that if the parents are prepared—and this does not work unless they are fully prepared—that it might be just as well to do the search earlier while the child still has the family as a holding environment.

The Hamiltons went to court and got permission to find out more about Patricia. At the time of the adoption, fourteen years before, they had only been given sketchy information, nothing substantial. At the time, it had seemed like more than enough to them. As Patricia grew and asked question after question, they began to wonder why they had not been given more information. Patricia needed to know.

Patricia's parents went to see the social worker who helps with searches at the Department of Social Services while their daughter was in school one day. The worker pulled the file on Patricia and told the parents a bit about her history. They learned that Patricia was the product of incest. Her mother is also her older sister. They were horrified and shocked. They shook their heads and said, "We certainly can't tell her this!"

The social worker suggested that the parents call my office and come in for a consultation on this complicated matter. The couple entered my office a few days later and said that they did not know why they were here. They stated that there was no way they were going to tell their daughter this horrible news. They would wait until she was eighteen or twenty-one to tell her.

I suggested to them that this was pretty difficult news to make sense of at any age. I asked if she was a "searcher." They said that she had never stopped asking. They said that this was the first year Patricia was doing well in school and they worried that she might be too upset by this news and not do well. I then suggested that perhaps we could first see if the birth mother was willing to be "found." Then we could think about videotaping a session with me interviewing her birth mother, sharing that video with the three of them, and then videotaping Patricia to show to her birth mother. This way we could buy some time for the rest of the school year. It was March.

Next, I saw Patricia with her parents. She was angry as she walked in, wanting to know who I was and why she had to go through all of these hoops to have information about herself that should belong to her. I suggested that her parents were supporting her search, but that they were worried about her concentration in school. She put her hands on her hips and said, "If they don't let me find her, they'll see school problems!"

I told Patricia that we sometimes do this video thing and asked what she thought about it. Surprisingly, she liked the idea. She said that she worried about how awkward it would be meeting the first time and not knowing each other and that she had been thinking, "If only I could just see her first." Patricia asked me to do the interview as if I were Barbara Walters, then Patricia proceeded to write the script.

Meanwhile, the DSS worker had contacted Wendy, the birth mother, to see if she was prepared and willing to meet with Patricia. Wendy said that she was thirteen years old when Patricia was born and that she had had drug and alcohol problems ever since. Three years ago, on Patricia's birthday, she had stopped drinking and doing drugs and had sought out help. Wendy was now in an incest support group. She was taking classes at a community college and working full-time. She felt very prepared and said that she had waited for this day.

Wendy came into the office first for the interview. It was incredible how much these two women looked alike. They are, after all, sisters as well as mother and child. We spent some time chatting first. Wendy said that she did not want to tell Patricia about the incest on video and that she would prefer to answer any questions about the birth father by saying that that information would wait for the actual meeting. I supported her in this very wise decision.

We then went into the video room and I began my Barbara Walters act. Patricia's script was carefully planned. The first question was easy, the next one hard, and so on. She asked about her favorite music, then she asked about family. Wendy shared that she had two younger brothers and a sister who had a baby and lived with her at present. The next question was about her favorite color or food, and then she asked about her parents. She stated that her mother lived nearby and was ill. Wendy sees her often. She said that she had not seen her father for thirteen years. The next question was about what she did for fun, and then came the dreaded question: "Who was my birth father?" Wendy said, "I'd rather wait to tell you that kind of information when we meet." The next question was, "Do you see him now? Do you know where he is?" Wendy said that she had not seen him for thirteen years.

After the video was made, Wendy and I talked for a while. I told her I would be showing the video to Patricia and her parents, and then Patricia would make one, which I would invite her back to see; then we would work toward an actual meeting. Wendy understood that Patricia needed to get through school.

Patricia and her parents came in to view the tape. Patricia was excited and nervous. We all sat in the room and I played the video. If I had been astounded to see the resemblance between Patricia and Wendy, you can imagine how Patricia felt—never having seen another birth relative. And how amazed her parents were, knowing the complicated relationship! We all sat and watched. At the end, the Hamiltons were stricken with worry about how Patricia was feeling. Patricia sat quietly and then she said, "I have this feeling . . . I think that my father is my grandfather." I asked, "Wendy says that she wants to wait to meet you to tell you who your birth father is. If that were true, what would it mean?" Patricia had her head in her hands and looked up and said, "How could someone do that to a kid?" I could see the Hamiltons relaxing as they realized that Patricia was more concerned about the injustice of what had happened.

To make a long story short, we did the other video and bought some time. Patricia passed the year and looked forward to the meeting with Wendy. At their meeting, Wendy told Patricia the story of her family and her life and how hard it had been but said she always knew she would meet Patricia someday and she wanted her to know that she was loved; Wendy told her she was only twelve when she got pregnant and had no choice, and that she knew that her family was not a good family for kids to grow up in.

Wendy basically wanted to be adopted by the Hamiltons. She started to call often and wanted to come over and hang out. Finally, Patricia had to put her foot down. She told Wendy, "I'm glad we've met and that we are building a relationship, but I just can't spend all of my time with you. I have friends and a boyfriend. I think it would be best if we saw each other about once a month or so." The Hamiltons ended up being worried about Wendy's feelings and called her in between.

At one point, the Hamiltons came into my office to discuss an argument they were having. Wendy wanted them to come to a barbecue to meet some of her family. John Hamilton was horrified. "I can't go and meet those people!" he said. His wife said, "You have to, doesn't he, Joyce?" I responded, "John, you're a sociologist! You have to go. First of all, Patricia has invited you. She needs you to witness this with her."

After the barbecue, the Hamiltons came back in. I asked John if it was as bad as he thought and he said, "Worse, but I'm so glad I went." That didn't sound like it made sense. John then said that he had always had his own projections about how Patricia should be. And when he saw how strong she was throughout the reunion he had a new respect and admiration her.

Patricia was going to find out where she came from no matter what. Thank goodness she did it with the help and support of her parents. She found the strength to accept her past. Patricia was able to discover that Wendy was her birth mother, but that she was more like a sister or a special friend. Wendy had grown up in a family of incest and no boundaries. Patricia's boundaries were very good and she set them at every juncture as she needed to.

Time out

The Department of Social Services called us to do a consult on a difficult case. The Jones family had taken an infant directly from Children's Hospital. The baby was born with drug toxicity and was in fragile shape at the time of birth. The Joneses, Ella and Mac, had loved and cared for Dwayne until he was well, and now at age three he was a healthy and happy child. Dwayne's birth mother, Erika, had been in jail ever since his birth. Ella and Mac were told indirectly and directly by social workers that they would be able to adopt Dwayne, since his mother was not going to be able to parent him and had never seen him.

Erika was assigned a new lawyer, however, who was amazed that she had never had visits with her child, who was legally in foster care. The lawyer went through the necessary legal motions and gained, for her client, visits with her son.

When Dwayne went to the correctional institute with his social worker he would come back very upset. He was crying and acting out and wetting the bed. The Joneses desperately wanted the visits to stop.

I asked that all of the adults come in for a consultation. On the day scheduled, the childcare arrangement fell through, so Dwayne came, too, along with Ella and Mac; the social worker and her supervisor; the lawyer for Erika; and some of my team. Mac asked if he could wait outside with Dwayne and we said no. We explained to Dwayne that he could be in the room with us and play with the toys, but that he could only use two at a time and had to put them back. We also explained that he could interrupt (politely) and tell us anything or fix anything the adults were saying that was wrong.

Less than five minutes into the session, we asked who had explained to Dwayne who Erika was and what jail was. The social worker nodded in the direction of the foster parents and said, "I expect they told him." The foster parents said that they had not, that they had assumed the social worker had. So minutes into the session, we learned that no one had explained these things to the three-year-old. We asked Dwayne what he thought. He said he didn't know. We explained that Erika is his "tummy mommy," that he grew in her tummy but that she could not be a parent. So Ella and Mac are his parents and have been his mommy and daddy all along—ever since he left the hospital after he was born. He said, "Oh!" We then asked where he thought Erika was. He didn't know. We asked if he ever did anything bad and if he did how was he punished. He said he sometimes did bad things and that he had to go into time out and wait until he thought about what he did that was wrong. When he thought about it and could say sorry, he could come out. We explained that Erika was in Big Time Out, that she had done something grown-up bad and that in her time out she could not come out when she felt like it, but had to stay there until the judge told her she could leave. We explained that kids need parents every single day and explained again that although Erika was his birth mother, she had never been his parent.

The next time Dwayne went to jail to visit Erika, his foster parents accompanied him. They were nervous but understood that he needed people he knew and trusted with him. They said that they were surprised; they had had extremely negative feelings about Erika, but when they met her they found there were things that they liked about her. Dwayne took the opportunity to interview all the inmates about what they had done that was so bad that they were in Big Time Out!

✧

Not every family can tolerate the level of openness that both Patricia's family and Dwayne's family came to appreciate. We must work to help families to find their own level of openness and to recognize that this may change as the years go by. None of this can or should be forced upon people. If, however, an adoptive family decides it wants to have some kind of relationship with the birth mother it can work out very well not just for the adopted person, but for the entire family of adoption.

Even more than legal openness, I'm concerned about emotional openness in the family of adoption. I often see families with adolescents who are acting out in some way and parents who don't accept that they are all being affected by the issues that inevitably arise in an adoptive family. Although they may talk openly about adoption in general, they are rigid when they talk about it in terms of their own family. There's a sense of closedness which makes it difficult for the children to feel they can gain information about themselves without hurting their adoptive parents. These families are often committed to appearing as if they are a biologically related one. This is stressful and demeaning for the children, who know that this is not true.

David Kirk, in his book *Shared Fate,* talks about how the most healthy adoptive families are the ones in which there is acknowledgment of difference. The most difficult adoptive family situations, according to Kirk, are those in which there's absolutely no acknowledgment of difference. Many adoptive parents in our closed system were led to believe that the birth mother would just get on with her life and forget about this episode, and that the adoptive parents would have their baby and it would be as if they had never been infertile. But it wasn't like that. It's not necessarily bad-different or good-different, it's just different.

Adoptive parents often feel blamed for their children's confusion. When someone says, "Adoption is the problem," they hear, "You are the problem as the parent." We try to explain that the system of adoption is the problem, and that the parents are as much victims of that system as are the birth parents and the children. I'll let Penny Callan Partridge speak one last time in this book with "Daddy," a story that beautifully illustrates how much both adoptive child and parent can be harmed by a sense of closedness in the system of adoption.

> *I went home for Christmas knowing I wanted to talk, not just with my mother but with my parents together, about looking for my birthparents.*
> *The last time I had said anything to my father about adoption was more than twenty years earlier. We were walking out to the garage*

to get in the car and go on an errand. I said, "Daddy, I know my name was Dorothy Elizabeth before I was adopted, but what was my last name?" He started coughing his smoker's cough and didn't stop until I really thought maybe he was having a heart attack. I picture his spasms over the steering wheel, and then I picture us driving off down the street with me feeling like not opening my mouth ever again about anything.

But now I was concerned that my father was hearing about my search only through my mother. I was thirty. I ought to be able to say something to him directly about it. So after dinner one night, I told my parents that I wanted to talk to them together about something. The three of us arranged ourselves around the high-ceilinged living room of the Santa Barbara house my parents had moved to when I was in college.

"I want to talk to you about looking for my birthparents. I want you to know it's not that I want to replace you. I want to see people I look like."

My father harrumphed some. "Well, you should know that for awhile we weren't even planning to tell you you were adopted." What?! I couldn't remember ever not knowing I was adopted, and my mother had such a thing about truth telling and openness. Not telling me was probably less their plan than a hope he had had only until he voiced it to her.

"But what if she's gone on and married a senator, and you arrive at their house in the middle of a cocktail party? You could ruin this man's career!"

"Daddy! You're . . . my father! You're supposed to worry about ME—not some man you don't even know!"

And this man—possibly one of the world's least demonstrative human beings except with cats, to whom he talked with incredible sweetness and affection—came across the living room with arms open wide and I saw tears in his eyes. "Oh my dear! What can I do to help?"

That's how my father got it that I needed and wanted him as a father, EVEN though he wasn't my biological father, and EVEN though we were a hilarious match in some ways. When I went to social work school, he worried that it would probably lead to marrying a social worker. (It did!) He had wanted me to be a secretary so I'd be more likely to marry a businessman.

What a shame for both my father and me that he was my father for thirty years without really feeling it. But this is why I like to say that,

*among other things, my search for my birthparents got me my adoptive
father. An emotional channel was opened between us that had not been
there before. It's a good thing it got opened when it did, because my father
and I soon enough had my mother's sudden death and then his slow one
to go through together. We really needed each other.*

The search and the reunion

We all search for ourselves in various ways. We visit the ancestral lands
and homes of our grandparents. We look within us and around us to find
out who we are and what our purpose is. This is true for everyone. The
search for adopted people is thwarted by closed records and legal fictions—false birth certificates. As adopted children grow, they begin to
wonder more and more about the story of their lives. They may ask
questions, and often, as we've seen, their parents do not have answers.
If, at the time of the adoption, the parents had no desire for more information, they often feel differently later as their child begins asking more
and more questions. It is the right and responsibility of the parents to
find the information that will be the truth for that child and, as parents,
to convey it in ways that make sense to their child at his particular developmental stage. This is the search—all the questioning that leads up to
finding the birth family. The reunion is the actual meeting. A reunion is
not something one has a *right* to; people must respect the wishes of others. A reunion must not be forced. Sometimes the person who is found
is not as ready to meet as the searcher is and refuses a reunion. There are
people—birth parents, adoptive parents, professionals involved with
adoption—who are concerned about making original birth certificates
available to adopted people. They worry that the adopted person will in-
vade the privacy of the person who is found. Others believe, however,
that adults should have the right to approach each other in a respectful
way, and that they should at the same time understand and abide by
whatever boundaries the other person sets. There is no other situation
in this country in which adults do not have access to information
about themselves.

When parents of very young children want to open an adoption
that was closed, I believe that is their choice as adults, as parents. When
parents of adolescents want to support their children with a search, I

often suggest that the child "hire" them as administrative assistants and let them do the written and telephone work. It is important for the parents to be involved but for the children to feel in charge. There is sometimes a tendency for parents to go too far when that is not what the child had in mind. Remember, a search is not always a reunion.

After the search, when new information is available, it's often very difficult for the adopted person to give up the fantasy parent. The fears and hopes of the adopted person are that the birth mother is going to turn out to be a bag lady (this message regarding poor birth mothers is the one society's been giving them all along, after all), or some fairy tale person dazzlingly rich, famous, beautiful, kind. What one often finds is an ordinary person, and that is a huge disappointment.

I've been doing therapy with adopted people who have searched for over twenty years. I've seen some people find that their birth parents are now middle-aged, competent, middle-class people—not the adolescents without resources preserved in the birth records. I've seen some people find horrible, sad things. And yet the search has always been successful, because of the healing and connection it brings.

International search

International adoptions are very complicated situations when it comes to a search. What resolution is there for people for whom no search is possible?

Some parents can only say, "We know he was left on the street. We know the name that he gave the policeman when he was picked up, and we know that no birth records are available." Many children who are internationally adopted have no information about their origins, but they do have an identification with their birth country as opposed to their birth mother, and they need to have more help understanding things about their culture of birth. Just as some children repress any wondering about the birth mother, internationally adopted kids, on the surface, may not want to have anything to do with their birth country or birth culture. It is important in those cases for the adoptive parents to feel as if, and to convey that, they wish they knew more, too. For the parents to join the child in an honest way in this is important: to say, "You're so great. Your birth mother must have been wonderful too. I wonder what she looked like. I wonder what she would say if she saw you. I would really like to know more about your family of origin. You are a part of our family, and that makes them our extended family, too. I often wonder about them, and I often think of and thank your birth mother for allowing me to be your other mother. She understood that all children need to have a parent or parents, and she couldn't be that. If there is any way we can possibly learn more about your birth family, we will help you to do that."

In some cases, an international search seems nearly impossible. There are several adult adopted people I work with who were adopted as babies from Korea. There was a time when people assumed that the children adopted from Korea in the 1950s—our first real stream of international adoptions—would never know their birth parents. In fact, these adoptions were popular with some for exactly this reason. Many of these adoptees are now almost fifty years old. Some have gone back on a pilgrimage to Korea and to the orphanage listed on their birth records to pursue a search. They have told me that these trips are difficult— that they at first experience a feeling of homelessness much like that of a domestically adopted person who finds in the course of a search for her birth family that she doesn't wholly belong there, either. Except, for these adoptees searching in Korea, these feelings are magnified by the lack of familiarity with language, place, and culture and by the fact that, although they look Korean, they know they are not.

Over the years I have had the pleasure and honor to meet many Korean birth mothers (and also birth mothers from Colombia, El Salvador, Guatemala, Peru, and Romania). The Korean birth mothers talk about the historical perspective: how serious postwar poverty was, how traditional the country was, and how families were very closed. The Korean birth mothers taught me that these 1950s babies (much like the Chinese baby girls being adopted today) were not abandoned. The birth mothers waited behind a tree or nearby to watch after they had "placed" the child on a doorstep, to see that the right person took the child into keeping. To place the child on certain doorsteps guaranteed that the child would be taken to one of the many religious orphanages that then arranged for adoptions in other countries. Adoption was not an option within Korea. Recently, as a result of the international exchanges set in motion by the 1988 Olympics in Seoul, the country was made aware of its so-called Lost Children. Many Korean people are now working hard to provide the genealogical information and the connections that those children—many of whom are now adults—need to understand more about who they are. There are increasing numbers of people going to Korea to do searches, and there are increasing reunions. It is still a delicate process. The country has strong traditions concerning honor, and birth mothers are still filled with guilt and shame.

Families who are adopting from China today may feel sad that their children can never search. That is what we once said about Korea. But experience shows that things will change: advances in genetic matching and communication will make it increasingly possible to trace families of origin. Those Chinese birth parents know the exact place and day that they placed their baby on a hillside or at a church door, and they will know years hence, when perhaps an ad is placed in a local paper by the child they left, now searching for them. We cannot suppress the human need to be connected.

Epilogue
Adoption and beyond

Many years ago in Hawaii, I was one of two keynote speakers at a conference, both of us adopted. The gentleman went first. He was native Hawaiian, and in Hawaii there is an ancient custom of adoption called hanai. In a Hawaiian marriage, when you become "related" to the in-law family, you are then considered one family, and you would not "war" against each other. The same is true in hanai—if you place your child with another family, the two families become connected, and are considered one large extended family. This Hawaiian adopted person opened the conference with loud drums and chanting. It was beautiful—stunning—and it went on for quite a while. The entire audience sat very still and listened, mesmerized.

When he had finished, he stated that he had just recited the names of his ancestors. He had chanted the lineage of both his family by birth and his family by adoption. He said that it is a great honor to be a hanai person, as you are the reservoir that holds the lineage of two great families; you are the place and the person where they connect and become one extended family. It is a prestigious position to be the connector of two families.

This was an incredibly hard act to follow! When I got up to give my keynote speech, I dropped my original outline and talked instead about how wonderful it would be, in American culture, if adoption were an honor—if each adopted individual were held in such a revered and respected position, and in turn felt this pride and respect toward both sets of families.

In our culture, to this day, adoption is "second choice" (although not second best), and it is treated that way, not by the adoptive or birth families themselves, but by many people in the wider community, and often by the media. They may not like to admit it, but there are those in the general public who think it is unacceptable for a mother not to raise the children she has given birth to, whether it is her choice not to parent, or whether her children have been removed from her care.

Just as an adopted person often needs to search into his/her past to find the links that will be of help in building an integrated future, so does our society need to look at some of the ancient beliefs about family, and to integrate these traditions and insights into how we currently view and treat families by adoption.

Critical to a new way of viewing adoption is the understanding that adoption (or emotional adoption: placement in a foster family or in any other significant, life-altering family connection) is not an isolated event. It is a lifelong process and an intergenerational journey. As such, each member in the family nexus changes, and certain developmental transitions occur that need to be addressed with loving attention.

What if the general public took the time to put themselves in the shoes of an adopted person?

Think about it. It's hard enough to figure out who you are, and what your purpose is in life, if you are born and raised in one and the same family! When you are adopted, it is all that much more complicated. There is no judgment in this statement. Being an adopted person is just extremely complex.

For the adopted person who is in a closed adoption—domestic or international—there is, at some point, the realization and the truth that you do not know another human being in this whole wide world who is genetically related to you!

We humans are interrelated and interdependent beings. What would it be like not to know another human who is genetically related to you? Of course there are two ways that someone can fix this dilemma. He/she can search and find the birth family, the genetic relatives; or, he/she can make a baby and create a new set of genetic relatives.

The Winds of Change

Openness is finding its way into adoption. In 1993, a study by researcher Marianne Berry found that in 69 percent of public and private agency adoptions, the birth parents had met the adoptive couple.[1] In the years since that study, we can hypothesize that the numbers are growing. The

National Adoption Information Clearinghouse (NAIC) reports that almost every state had amended its adoption statutes to create complete anonymity by the early 1950s. Research conducted beginning in 1974 demonstrated that some of the psychological problems found in adolescent and adult adopted persons, birth parents, and adoptive parents appeared to be directly related to the secrecy, anonymity, and sealed records of closed adoption.

Fortunately, open adoption has become increasingly common since the 1970s, when research and practice began promoting the principles of open adoption.[2] As of 2004, there are fifteen states with some form of Access to Birth Certificates, and seven of those changed their laws in the last seven years. There is legislation pending in some twenty-one other states as well.

Adopted people are the only citizens of the United States who do not have access to their original—and only true—birth certificates. This is a civil right. It is encouraging that states are passing legislation that gives adoptive parents access to their child's original birth certificate; further, if the parents do not choose to share it with the child, he / she has the right to access it at age of maturity (ages eighteen to twenty-one, depending on the state).

Adoption frequently imposes a negative identity image on the child—and then the adult adopted person—when secrecy is its foundation, and lack of trust is a partner to that secrecy. This is not the doing of the adoptive parents or the birth parents. It is the system of adoption, and our society as a whole that creates this problem. The problem also lies with some of the professionals in the system whose personal bias and beliefs are based on a past and therefore preclude their serving this population with sensitivity and understanding.

The National Adoption Information Clearinghouse (NAIC), a service of the Children's Bureau of the U.S. Department of Health and Human Services (DHHS) Administration of Children and Families, has a wealth of information about many aspects of adoption. In their recent Fact Sheet for Families on Openness in Adoption they discuss the various levels of openness in adoption, and talk about the goals of open adoption:

- To minimize the child's loss of relationships.
- To maintain and celebrate the adopted child's connections with *all* of the important people in his / her life.

• To allow the child to resolve losses with the truth, rather than the fantasy adopted children create when no information about or contact with their birth family is available.

Adoption is intergenerational. It lasts a lifetime and beyond. It not only affects the families of the birth parents and the adoptive parents, but it has an impact on future generations as well. Often, when an adopted person has not done an inner search, or a search for origins, the children of that adopted person become the searchers. It is their legacy as well. The winds of change blow into the next generation. I was moved by the following essay written by an eighteen-year-old woman named Kelley McGee, whose father is adopted.

From a Daughter's Perspective

I am one-eighth Swedish, one-eighth Irish, one-quarter Italian, and one-half adopted. On my mother's side I can trace my roots back to the boat that came over from Sicily and the passage that all of my ancestors took through Ellis Island. On my father's side there's a letter from the Spence-Chaplin adoption agency, in New York City, describing my father's genealogy. A piece of paper is all that links me to half of my "vital information" or however the bureaucracy wants to phrase it. I'm guessing that I'm half a person in a sense, but does that make my father not even one?

My dad is searching for his birth mother. He has every right to know who he is, but that's not to say he doesn't still love and respect everything about his adoptive parents. They are the only people he's ever had to call mom and dad and that I had the honor of calling nanny and poppop. They were great people. My father grew up in a very privileged home. Maybe he might not have had that kind of life with his "real" mother, but he was never given the chance to be with her.

Many are quick to say that since my father was adopted at such a young age, he shouldn't know the difference. Fifty-one years ago, nine months of bonding were shared between a mother and the child in the womb. They were one unit, my father living off of her life. Then at the tender age of three weeks old he was given away to new people. These were people who would love him more than anything in the whole world, but people with whom he would never share that bond.

It is now being called a "primal wound"—the severing of all ties with the person who gave birth to him. It is a sense of loss that is almost incomprehensible. I could only imagine the pain my father was going through until I accompanied him to his weekly support group meeting in New York City. Here was a room full of people who felt like they didn't even exist or that they were aliens in a land where everyone else had what they never could. I'm sure that they all have their own baby pictures but who is there to tell them about the day they were born? Who is there to tell them that they kicked a lot at night?

Who can say that they were there for the very moment that the person was brought into the world? Who can prove where they came from? No one.

I have half of these feelings. I know that it was icy the day I was born. I know that my mother remembers me kicking hard and what that was like. I have seen the pictures of me, brand new in my hospital crib. I have two parents and had four grandparents who could account for the miracle of me being born. All my dad had is that letter and in turn all that I have is half a past.

So where does my family go from here and why am I so deeply affected by all of this? As of now, the only blood ties that my father has are me and my sister and you can bet that he hangs on tightly. Hopefully one day he'll get to meet his mother. Maybe one day he'll be able to look into the eyes of his mother and see where he came from. As for me, all I can do is be totally supportive of everything that my father is doing. I believe in his search—not only for his sake, but for my own. It's not just my father's roots—they're mine too. I want to know where my blond hair comes from. I want to know if I have an aunt that looks just like me or maybe, even, that looks just like my grandmother. I may never get to know any of this and I accept that.

Questions still linger in my mind. They hang there poised and ready, filled with frustration, anger, and a sense of helplessness. Why did it have to be like this? Were the relationships that all this has formed and the love that people have shared worth the pain it's causing now? Maybe these are all unanswerable questions. Maybe this whole thing is a gigantic puzzle that was never meant to be solved. Maybe it is an act of fate. Maybe my father was destined to live a life that his mother couldn't give him and we may just have to accept that without ever knowing why.

Sensitivity and Competence in Adoption

The estimated total number of adoptions in the United States has ranged from a low of 50,000 in 1944 to a high of 175,000 in 1970.[3] In general, it's fair to say that there are approximately 120,000 adoptions per year, and that this number has remained fairly constant.[4]

According to Flango and Flango, 15.5 percent of adoptions (19,753) were from public agencies; 37.5 percent (47,627) were private, independent, or non-agency—children placed in non-relative homes directly by birth parents, or through the services of licensed or unlicensed facilitators, certified medical doctors, members of the clergy, or attorneys. Stepparent adoptions were 42 percent (53,525). International adoptions counted for 5 percent (6,536)—in 1997 that number increased to 13,620. The numbers of children placed in relatives' homes with or without the services of a public agency are not as well known.

A recent report from the Census Bureau showed that 1.6 million adopted children under age 18 live in U.S. households. Although international adoptions are increasing, 87 percent of these adopted children were born in the United States. Seventeen percent are of a different race than the head of household. Among the foreign-born, 49 percent come from Asia, with Korea leading the list. These adopted children tend to live with older and more economically secure parents.

Adoptive families are fairly evenly distributed across the USA. In the United States, 92.5 percent of all children live with a biological parent, 5 percent live with a stepparent, and 2.5 percent live with an adoptive parent. About 126,000 children are in foster care and are eligible for adoption; the average age of these children is eight.[5] The Evan B. Donaldson Institute did a study in 1997 that revealed that 52 percent of Americans interviewed had a direct connection to adoption (adopted persons, birth parents, adoptive parents, etc.).[6]

I think this makes it very clear that we need to spend more time and money educating the American public about adoption.

If international adoptions were done with a clear and serious understanding of the child's need to respect and connect with his/her culture, race, and ethnicity—as well as that of the adoptive family—and if we aimed to make resources available for the adoptive parents to share with the child as he/she grew, then we would be striving to create only

the best and most healthy adoptions. Adoption is a very interesting social construction, and it creates a very different understanding of who is
in a family. Adoption shows us that families are not only related by
blood, but also by choice and by chance.

The children waiting for adoption in our own country sometimes have the advantages of good prenatal care, good nutrition, and being part of an extended community, by virtue of sharing a country of origin. The conditions of international adoption can vary. Fifteen years
ago, over two-thirds of international adoptions were from Korea (where
there is a good standard of living, as well as foster homes and excellent
health care). Now, however, three-quarters of our children adopted internationally are arriving from countries that rely on institutional care,
have a low per-capita income, and provide inade quate nutrition and
health care.[7] This means that pre-adoptive parents must be even better
informed and better prepared for these international adoptions, and
that competent post-adoption services must be available.

There are certainly ways to educate people, and to dispel myths
and fears that the birth families (or birth countries) are bad, dangerous,
and unsafe for the child, and should not be part of his/her life. There is
a small percentage of cases where the danger may be real, and in these
cases the child should certainly be protected, but—even then—not
from everyone in his/her family of origin.

Apparently many professionals do not truly believe that the need
to honor our connections is an essential part of family life, as this belief
is not reflected in the way that they work with families in stress who are
dealing with complex issues of foster care, guardianship, kinship, and
adoption. Whether it was a closed or open adoption, an adopted child
must learn to integrate at least two distinctly different families—the
birth family and the adoptive family. The biracial or other-culture child
must also integrate two distinctly different cultures. The challenge to
adoptive parents, and to others connected to this child, is to help the
child to develop his/her own identity within the framework of both
cultures.

The challenge to professionals is to help the whole family to see
itself as a multicultural family, and to develop its identity while integrat-
ing—not ignoring—the distinctively different cultures.

How can that happen if the professionals don't see the importance of respect for culture? How can that happen if the professionals don't see any difference in culture because the race is the same? The psycho-education and modeling done by the professionals who are initially involved in building these complex families can set a tone, and begin a process of respect and integration. Without this education and modeling, the parents might be so busy with other essential psychological and emotional issues, and with possible trauma management for this child, that they might ignore the very important issues of culture and development of identity. Without that awareness, how will the parents be prepared to model and teach the larger community—the schools, courts, religious institutions, and neighborhoods—thereby creating a holding environment for that child that both honors and respects all of who he / she is?

What Adoption Professionals and Policy Makers Need to Know

•   That training in preparation, mediation, and prevention is essential for all professionals working in adoption. I would recommend training professionals to *work as a team,* which would then serve as a model for the families to work as a team, in the very best interest of the child.
•   That the problems that exist for children in foster care today exist right up the chain of the administration that serves them. Professionals should be aware of their own personal feelings of insecurity (about the salient issues in adoption), confusion about their roles, manipulation, and fear of loss or change that is also replicated in the system as a whole. These problems, as they are played out by the government, the agencies, workers, caretakers, parents, and other adults, do not give a child much hope for change.
•   That we must make changes from the top down *and* from the bottom up, if change is to be real and sustaining. This process will take a very long time, but, in the best interest of the children, we must begin the process at every level and at this very moment.
•   That there is a need for competent counseling and planning, and that it must be a collaborative effort among private clinicians, mental health centers, lawyers, clergy, educators, and other professionals who influence the planning and decisions that are made for the child. Unless

mediation is done to make sure that the parties involved are working together for the very best interest of the child, there is an adversarial feeling that greatly affects the outcome of each and every case.

• That *all* cases should involve concurrent planning with birth parents, birth family, and extended kin, along with potential outside foster and/or adoptive families. The professional parties, both public and private, must have some perspective to view this collaboration as a way of preserving the important knowledge that all of these professionals bring to the life of each and every child and family. This work should not be seen as simply a depletion of resources.

• That mediation, or systemic work, with the public and private agencies that are granted the right and privilege to work with these families *must* be a part of the plan to heal the whole system.

• That post-placement services and post-adoptive services should never be ignored. If families have support and mediation at various stages, and if they have the understanding that their difficulties are normal (after all, adopted children often have been abused and neglected—there is trauma involved), then they will have the stamina to stay involved when times are tough. The NAIC states that post-adoption services are not an "extra," but are a critical ingredient of a successful adoption.

• That these families will often require support and services. Without these services these may *not* be permanent plans for these children. Many professionals believe there is a correlation among poor placement planning, lack of ongoing services, and disruption or dissolution in adoption and other so-called "permanent plans" for the children in this system.

• That unifying adoption (not standardizing it) is important, and should be addressed. Adoption has many different forms—private, public, international, trans-racial, foster/adopt, guardian, kinship, open, and closed. There should be some unification of the understanding of what adoption *is* and what it *is not*.

• That as part of this unification, there should be limits placed on the amounts of money charged in private domestic and international adoption, and more money in the larger pool of adoption monies, granted for post-adoption as a way to provide families and children with post-adoption security and safety while preserving their cultural, religious, racial, and/or ethnic ties.

Ways to Unify Adoption

• Education of the general public about what adoption is and what it is not, and education about what adopted children and adoptive families need from their communities in order to be supported.

• Cooperation between public and private agencies throughout the process of adoption, as well as clarification of roles and responsibilities. Being clear about the roles played by professionals will help clarify the roles of parents: birth, foster, or adoptive. An adversarial approach and competition to *own* services replicates the adversarial approach and competition to *own* the child. These approaches have not worked, and will not work, for the agencies or for the families—and, most important, they will not work for the child.

• Review of Home Study Process. In the 1940s and 1950s these were truly "home" studies. Today, with the complex situations we face, and with the need for a diversity of placements for a diverse population of kids and families, we need to be doing "family studies," not "home studies." I would recommend two levels to a family study. The first level would put the parent(s) in the pool of people who are generally ready and responsible, who could be considered as parents. A very large number of pre-adoptive parents are, of course, approved in general as part of their required home study. The second level would be a determination of which child would be best served by being placed in this particular family. We have lost the ability, in both public and private adoptions, to see who would be *the best family for a child,* and we often make placements in the best interest of the family. The family should be able to put themselves and their egos aside to look at what would be best for the child—not just in this moment in time, but for the child's entire life. This would not only be in the best interest of the child, but ultimately for that family as well.

• Development of a team of public/private and court professionals who will follow a particular case, making sure that services are not duplicated and that all of the supports and services necessary to provide permanency for that child and family are made available. The team should report to *one* judge throughout the process.

• Prevent disruptions by realizing that many families have complex issues, and will need extensive services for their child(ren)—sometimes including hospitalization or residential care. Residential placement does not have to mean that the family is disrupted. It can mean that the child and family in crisis are in need of extended services, and that they must all join together with the service agency to continue to provide the child with a feeling of continuity of care—even if he/she is not able to live in the home.

•　　Have the team work to develop goals and *plans for each child,* and have those goals and plans assessed and reviewed at intervals that make sense in developing a lifelong plan for the child.

•　　Ask more of the adults who are interested in adopting older children. Rather than having the child's privacy impinged upon in newspapers and at adoption fairs, have the adults put themselves in a position where the child and his/her social worker can assess the family and make a good choice for that particular child. If a child over nine years old feels he/she is making a choice, the adoption will result in better attachment and will be more likely to be permanent.

System Changes Needed in Adoption

•　　Removing public agencies from voluntary adoption placements and shifting that function to the private sector, in order to conserve valuable public personnel resources, cut costs, and avoid duplication of services, can only be truly effective if the personnel in the private sector are trained in child welfare, social work, and family systems. Many private agencies and placement coordinators in our country are lawyers or facilitators who have no background in child development, child welfare, or family systems. Some are in the business of adoption simply because of personal concern and care. This is not enough. Our children deserve more.

•　　If we are to merge all adoptions (public, private, domestic, international, in-race, trans-racial, etc.)—and not have a caste system of rich and poor—we must give more attention, from the very beginning, to the larger issues that happen pre- and post-placement. As we can see, all of the contested adoption cases in the news almost always involve a lack of counseling, a lack of child welfare involvement, and a lack of education about the world of adoption.

•　　Privatize the adoption units of large public agencies; require licensing of private adoption services; and privatize relative/kin adoptions. All adoptions will only be successful if respect and mediation help to preserve the relationships and clarify the roles of family members.

Divided loyalty and loss of self-esteem due to family feuds is a problem that can and should be avoided, with the help of good preparation for a transfer of the parenting role within an extended family. It would be best if, during the first "temporary" foster situation when the child is removed from the home, the agency made an all-out effort to locate and identify relatives and friends/family. Without this very real effort, there is often contestation later, which is not in the best interest of anyone involved—and certainly not in the best interest of the child.

• Require interstate/international cooperation in early relative assessments. Allow public agencies to choose to assign the assessments to a private agency. This may save time and money, and help to produce timely reports to the public agency and the court for decision-making.

What Makes for Successful Adoptions

• Full disclosure of medical, developmental, and educational records, and other information on the history of the adopted child should always be made to adoptive parents. In order to make good plans for the child, it is essential that the family be given all of the information they need. If we were to do this in the best possible way, in terms of the human rights and civil rights of each child, we would do away with closed adoptions as we know them, and make decisions case by case about what level of openness would be safe and secure, and how families would get the support they need to maintain boundaries while preserving openness. All adoptions would include some semi-open facets, but of course not all adoptions would be fully open. There would be some situations where that would not be in the best interest of the child.

• The agency or adoption professional could act as an intermediary to keep a flow of communication. Medical information would be updated, and information—non-identifying, unless otherwise arranged by all parties—would be made available when requested. Medical history changes over time, as does the awareness of other information within a family. If there were to be some ongoing connection—to be determined within each case—it would lead to healthier decision-making and more autonomy on the part of the adoptive family. Remember— the *legal* adoptive parents are *the parents* of that child and should be able to make the best decisions as time goes on.

• Many parents, at some point, need information that was not available or did not seem important to them at the time of the legal adoption. Some private adoption practitioners fear that this kind of disclosure will hurt their adoption business. We have seen that this is not true, as the private adoption industry has gone from closed to semi-open, and as independent adoptions have flourished in this country in the past five to ten years.

• We must be wary of the "business" of adoption—lobbying and working against the best interest of the children and families that we are here to serve and to support.

• Temporary and foster or foster/adopt family. With regard to kinship adoption, and all other adoptions, it is important that the *original/ emergency foster placement of a child be temporary,* and that those parents be part of a team that will work together with the birth family, kin connections, and professionals to determine—as quickly as possible—whether the child will be moved to a kin placement, or moved to another foster family that has been determined to be an appropriate family for that particular child, should the placement become permanent. *All* parents in this position should know that in fostering a child, providing a bridge family, and making a permanent kinship connection, they are doing a great deal to foster health and healing. If they should become the permanent family of that child, they will have understood the need for the more positive connections to birth family and community. If they should be a bridge to a placement with birth parents or kin, they should be honored and respected as extended family in that process, having played an integral role in providing safety and continuity for that child.

• There should be no "legal risk" to the child waiting to be adopted. The only true risk occurs when the adults cannot work together in the very best interest of that child. At that point, the fragile emotional connections that a child requires in order to become a trusting adult are at great risk.

• The court process. Attorneys and judges need training to understand not only the legal issues involved, but the pre- and post-adoption issues that are an ongoing and central theme for all of the people involved in the adoption. Adoption is not a single event. It is a lifelong process. The attorneys and judges *need to have a framework* within which they can understand why one placement decision means real permanence. Adoption may be a venue for permanence, but if an adoption fails down the line because it was done without long-term goals and thinking, then it results in the same emotional cutoff and potential attachment problems that our faulty foster care system has created for the child. *Systemic thinking with both a child focus and a family focus is essential.*

•   All professionals must work together to expedite the best plans for permanence for each and every child. Attorneys must be part of the mediation, counseling, and consulting that take place en route to adoption. Attorneys and judges must be better equipped to understand what open adoption is and what it is not, so that they can guide families in clarifying their roles and responsibilities in the best interest of every child.

•   Open adoption is not joint custody. Parental rights are transferred, but relationships can be maintained, with roles and responsibilities changed and enunciated.

•   Adopted people in therapy sometimes discuss the slave-like feeling of having been bought and sold. They talk about the fact that some children "cost" more than others, and that there is a very real business of adoption that sometimes makes an adopted person feel as if he / she is a possession. This is not what the families are doing or expressing to the child, it is what the media is doing and expressing.

❖

Rather than advertise for families and for children, the first level of education for the general public should be an overview and understanding of adoption. We must change the thinking and understanding of the general public. We must de-pathologize some of the issues and concerns that are quite normal and to be expected in adoptive families. We must normalize the fact that families extend and include in various ways. We should make it respectable to be an adopted person.

Before we advertise for families, and become too business oriented, we must do our homework to educate people about systemic problems, about child-welfare issues, and about the strategies and strengths that a family must have to extend itself in this very special and wonderful way.

And finally, my mantra—

Adoption is not about finding children for families,
but about finding families for children.

❖

These thoughts are from a person who has been living in the world of adoption for nearly sixty years. I was adopted at ten days of age. I had a loving and good family, and we all struggled with issues that, in those days, we had no help to identify as normal within adoption. I have now known my birth family longer than I did not know them, and I truly love and respect *both* of my families. I feel the honor and the value of being the connecting point between these two families.

I have had over thirty years of experience as a professional in the world of adoption and have founded many centers, programs, and clinics that have helped to develop models for training and models of treatment of families challenged with the very complex issues that are a normal part of the adoption, foster, guardian, and kin family.

I have dedicated my life to adoption, and I am honored to have a voice in helping people to understand something more about the very extended and ever enlarging family of adoption.

Notes

1. M. Berry, "Risks and Benefits of Open Adoption," *Future of Children* 3 (1993): 125–138.

2. A. Baran and Reuben Pannor, "Perspective in Open Adoption," *Future of Children* 3 (1993): 199–124.

3. P. L. Maza, "Adoption Trends: 1944–1975," *Child Welfare Research Notes* 9 (1984).

4. V. Flango and C. Flango, *The Flow of Adoption Information from the States* (Williamsburg, VA: National Center for State Courts, 1994).

5. K. S. Peterson, "Census Counts Adoptees: 1.6M Kids," *USA Today,* 2 September 2003.

6. Evan B. Donaldson Institute, *Benchmark Adoption Survey: Report on the Findings* (New York: Evan B. Donaldson Institute, 1997).

7. D. E. Johnson, "International Adoption: New Kids, New Challenges," *Pediatric Basics* 94 (2001).

Adoption glossary

The definition of adoption, according to Webster's, is "A ready taking up of something." To adopt is (1) To take into one's family through legal means and raise as one's own child. (2) (a) To take and follow (a course of action, for example) by choice or assent. (b) To take up and make one's own. (3) To take on or assume.

In my work, I have found adoption to mean different things to different people:

> To some, adoption is the act of adoption—the legal moment in the courthouse.
> To some it is the life of adoption that the adopted child lives.
> To some it is the life of adoption that the adoptive parents live.
> To some it is the life of adoption that the birth parents live.
> To some it is the adoptive family, inclusive of the child.
> To some it is the extended family of adoption, including the birth parents (whether they are known or unknown, present or not).
> To a child, adoption is about being with the family they are in.

Sometimes, as I've said in chapter 3, when asked if they think about adoption, children say "no," and they are being honest. Children do, however, think about their birth family and wonder who they themselves are and where they came from. They do not see that as thinking about "adoption" while they are young and at a developmental stage of concrete thinking.

It is important that we think of *all* the people involved in adoption when making law and policy; and when developing treatment plans for families and training programs for both professionals and families. If we do not, we are not serving the larger community of adoption.

In an attempt to define various kinds of adoption, I give you the following list. No matter how sensitive one is to what one knows, things are often left out. I am prepared to have people write or call after reading this and say "you forgot . . .": And they will be quite right.

I've also added, at the end of this glossary, (several) legal terms and documents that relate to adoption.

Public adoption

In two U.S. states (Massachusetts and Connecticut), public adoptions are regulated by DSS or Child and Family Services, which require training in child welfare. In every state, public adoption services are available, either through a *public child welfare agency,* such as the Department of Social Services, Bureau of Children, or Child Welfare Agency, or through a *private child welfare agency,* such as Jewish Family and Children's Services, Catholic Charities, Lutheran Children's Services, or Casey Family Services.

Private adoption

In all but the two states that require the involvement of child welfare agencies in adoptions, lawyers and business people—some very good and ethical, and some simply in business—can arrange adoptions privately. Attorneys are often the ones who facilitate adoption. The adoption is then legalized in court.

In the forty-eight states that support private adoption, social workers, adoptive parents, or business people can decide to do adoptions and open private adoption businesses.

Independent adoption

In all of our states, more and more frequently, birth parents want to have some say in who adopts their child. The birth parents are involved in choosing and then meeting with the preadoptive couple or person who will eventually parent the child. Sometimes, couples who want to adopt put ads in papers and send letters to their friends, clergy, and physicians asking for the referral of a mother who has decided to place her baby for adoption.

Increasingly, then, the people involved in adoption are making their own arrangements and calling in the professionals only for the legal paperwork and finalization of their plans. When the parties involved have the best adoption counseling to make a good plan, not only for now, but for a lifetime, this route to adoption can be empowering for all parties. Without the proper guidance, however, independent adoptions can involve manipulation on the part of birth parents, adoptive parents, or attorneys or others involved. Independent adoptions that do not include education and counseling, and are not done with sensitivity and honesty, too often result in ill feelings and adoption disruption.

Closed adoption

A closed adoption is one in which the birth parents and adoptive parents know little or nothing about one another and have no identifying information. A large number of public and private adoptions are closed (educated guess: 45%). Most international adoptions are closed in the receiving country, but not in the sending country. In all adoptions, as stated earlier, sealed records are said to protect. When a contract—any contract—is made, all parties are supposed to agree and sign. In the case of adoption, though, the infant or child is not old enough to agree to this closed arrangement.

In the United States, records are still closed in all but three states (Kansas, Alaska, and Tennessee). This is not true in the United Kingdom, Australia, New Zealand, and in many other countries, where open records are a fact and where, when the child is not endangered, some form of open adoption is the usual practice.

Semi-open adoption

In a semi-open adoption, the birth and preadoptive parents meet once, without exchanging last names or addresses, and usually agree to send letters and pictures through an intermediary for a period of time. There is no agreement to any face-to-face contact or long-range connection other than an acknowledgment that the child will probably search for his birth parents when he becomes an older adolescent or adult.

Today, a high proportion of adoptions are semi-open. If the intermediary arrangement is working properly, so that if there is a hiatus in communication, the two parties can later reconnect through the intermediary, then, for instance, the adoptive parents and pediatrician can be kept informed of any medical information concerning the child. A semi-open plan can also become more open if both parties have developed a level of trust and are comfortable with that arrangement. Semi-open adoption often makes the growing child or adolescent feel left out, since it's only the adults who all seem to know one another.

Open adoption

Open adoption is not joint custody. Open adoption is an arrangement agreed to by the adoptive parents and birth parents in which there is an ongoing connection between them, to be determined by the parties involved. The birth parents still sign terminations of parental rights, and the adoptive parents become the full and legal parents of the child.

Open adoption ranges from what some people call open, but is actually semi-open, to a full relationship with ongoing connection and visits. Openness often varies over time, depending on the needs of the child and the parents' understanding of their roles and responsibilities. The success of open adoption depends on clear boundaries, the participants' respect for each other's roles and responsibilities, and the ability of the adults involved to put their egos aside in order to do what is best for the child.

Legal adoption

Legal adoption occurs when the birth parents' parental rights have been terminated via a Termination of Parental Rights (TPR) and the adoptive parents have taken on those parental rights through legal adoption proceedings.

Emotional adoption

There are some adoptive situations in which a child is raised by people who love and consider that child to be their own, and it is clear that there is a parent-child relationship, though it has not been legalized. This is often true in kinship arrangements (a grandmother parenting a grandchild), guardianships, and long-term foster care situations.

Infant adoption: same race

Most of the business of adoption, with private agencies, private attorneys, and adoption professionals, is same-race adoption, most commonly of a white infant by an infertile couple who want a child as much like the child they might have had as possible.

Same-race infant adoption is often done to keep a child who cannot stay in his birth family or extended birth family in his community of origin. Native American, Latino, Asian, Caucasian, and African American children are placed in families of the same ethnicity and culture when possible to give them a sense of community and connectedness.

If we are, in fact, looking for families for children, and not children for families, then adoption placement based on community or culture and ethnicity is the next best stage of connectedness.

Infant adoption: transracial

When all reasonable efforts have been made to keep the child with the birth family or within the same ethnic community, transracial adoption is a positive solution. Children *do* need families that are permanent and cannot be left in transitional homes for most, or all, of their childhood. This, unfortunately, has been done for too long in the foster care system in this country, a system that is a national disaster. We all want children to have the option of being in their families of origin or communities of origin as a first choice, but if that is not feasible at the time a child needs a family, then we must look for other families that can provide permanency and safety for the child.

In a transracial adoption, it is crucial, needless to say, that the family adopting a child of another race is sensitive to racism and has respect for their child's ethnicity and culture of origin.

The family must be willing to see itself as a transracial family, not to see the child as of another race.

The family should be willing to consider living in a diverse community so that the child can become familiar with and positive about his or her own culture, ethnicity, and racial background and can have positive adult role models of the same race.

Infant adoption: international

Infant adoptions from other countries are often transracial as well, so the same issues apply. Most common today in the United States are Chinese infant adoptions.

It is important for adoptive families to have respect for and an understanding of their child's country of origin. It is also important for agencies doing international adoptions to work with the sending countries and bureaus to make sure that as much information as possible is transmitted to the adoptive family so that they will have it when the child is older and asking questions.

How we talk to internationally adopted children about the complex societal issues involved in their adoptions is important; I discuss it further in terms of the developmental issues families face.

Older child adoption

Because of my interest in normalizing adoption, I am reluctant to say that there are special needs in all adoptions, but this is in a sense true. Adoption calls upon children to make sense of fundamental issues concerning identity and origin early on, and the process requires special treatment.

There is loss and trauma—the leaving of the birth mother and the move to another place—associated with all adoptions. For older children who are adopted, the trauma too often has been multiple and cumulative. The Child Welfare League of America has stated that 98% of the children over age three, both nationally and internationally, who are available for adoption have suffered sexual abuse, physical abuse, or neglect before being freed for adoption. This amount of early trauma is very important to detect and to understand. It used to be—and sometimes still is today—that parents were shielded from knowing about their children's trauma. This is certainly not in anyone's best interest.

The issues for the older child adopted from another race and culture are even more complex. There is the task of making sense of why no one in their family or in their community or country wanted them. Original language loss and new language acquisition for older children impacts their auditory processing and learning styles. In all older child adoptions, it is important to work to preserve positive connections in a safe and healing fashion.

Sibling adoption

Most child welfare professionals agree heartily that siblings should be kept together and adopted into the same family; this is what we mean by sibling adoption. All efforts are made to keep siblings together in public adoption. This is not as true in private adoption, in which siblings may be placed in separate households. In these cases, an open arrangement and commitment should be made between the two (or more) families to view themselves as extended family, so that the children can have some sense of ongoing family. This is important for their healing and growth. Giving a sense of continuity to siblings adopted into different families who are nevertheless willing to function as extended family is more possible in the case of domestic sibling adoption than it is in the more complicated international sibling adoption.

Kinship adoption

Kinship adoption means the adoption of a child by a grandparent, aunt or uncle, or other member of the extended family or by someone considered kin by the family, such as a dear old friend, called aunt or uncle, or a godparent. Many kinship adoptions are emotional, but not legal adoptions. This has been quite common for centuries.

Open kinship adoption refers to a kinship adoption of any of the kinds described above in which the roles and relationships are talked about and are clear. A *closed kinship adoption* is one in which the child is not told the truth concerning her birth parent. Very often sooner or later in life she discovers the truth from a family member.

Guardianship

Many families make legal guardianship plans for a child should the parents die or become incapacitated. Sometimes, in the case of older children, it makes more emotional and practical sense to have a plan for guardianship rather than adoption. Guardianship does not require parental rights to be severed or the child's name to be changed, although both of these might happen in the process.

Stand-by guardianship refers to a guardianship plan that is agreed to but not yet in effect. This newer form of guardianship was instituted because of the large number of children who have parents with a chronic disease who are unsure how long they will live. Parents who are HIV positive or who have progressing cancer often make plans for a family member or close friend to be available to step in during the serious phases of the illness when the parent will not be able to act as a parent. The plan is to slowly prepare the child and the guardian adult who will eventually be the parent figure. When these plans are made and talked about, both the child and the close friend or family member who will become guardian feel they are given permission, by the dying parent, to be together, in his or her absence, as a family.

Foster care

In our country, foster care is a system of care for children who have lost or been taken away from their parents and become "wards of the state." The government is their legal guardian. Volunteer foster parents, who are first screened and sometimes trained, care for these children and try to give them the normalcy of family life.

Temporary foster care

Most situations that require the removal of children from their homes and families are extremely traumatic and involve severe neglect and/or abuse. Children are often taken into emergency custody under a care and protection act and placed in any available foster home. Families who will do true temporary foster care are essential and much needed.

While a child is in temporary foster care, the social workers should be making every effort to find a safe and loving place for the child for the longer term, if the parents remain unfit to care for the child. Temporary foster care, in many instances, has turned by default into long-term and then permanent care. These days over half of the children in so-called temporary placement become adopted by those families.

All foster parents should know that in fostering a child they are doing a great deal to foster health and healing. If they should become the permanent family, they will understand the child's need for positive connections to her birth family and community. If they should be a bridge to a placement with kin or a return to the birth parents, they will often be honored as extended family.

Foster adoption

A high percentage (possibly half) of children in foster care are eventually adopted by their foster parents. Since this is the case, we must make a better effort to assure that foster care placement is child-specific and not virtually random.

Many foster parents who are on an adoption track from the beginning are told that the child is all but theirs although the parents' rights have not yet been terminated. These situations are referred to as "legal risk" adoptions. There should be no "legal risk." The only risk involved is that the fragile emotional connections that a child needs to form to become a trusting adult are at risk if all of the adults cannot work together in the best interest of that child.

Specialized/therapeutic foster care

In situations where a child has very special needs, a well-trained, professionally based foster home still may be the better alternative to a residential setting. Most often, specialized and therapeutic homes are clinical and temporary placements en route to a permanent plan. Most adoption agencies do not develop lasting connections for these children and their new families to these specialized homes, which can supply valuable mentorship and support even after the child has left.

Residential care

Children in residential care live with full-time house parents and aides in a boarding-school-like setting; all services are provided on campus. They attend school either on campus (for those with more special needs) or in the nearby school system. There is a highly therapeutic component to the time spent in the residential setting. Many children who have been severely neglected and traumatized need the kind of hourly coverage, daily therapy, and clinical services that only residential care provides.

Short-term residential care

During an acute crisis, to stabilize medications or dangerous behaviors, a brief stay in a residential center can be a therapeutic and necessary respite for the child or adolescent. An assessment can be done and recommendations made for the best treatment and education plan for the child.

Long-term residential care

For some severely traumatized children, the intimacy of a family and home would exacerbate posttraumatic reactions. Children in danger of abusing themselves or others need the long-term supervision of a residential setting.

Half adoption

When a partner in a couple adopts the birth child of the other partner, that child has been half adopted.

Donor recipient family

Donor sperm and donor egg families often fall into the old pattern of secrecy surrounding adoption. Similar issues to those dealt with in adoptive families present themselves for these complex families when there is an emotional, but not a legal, half adoption on the part of the parent whose sperm or egg was not involved. At times, in heterosexual couples, the idea of the donor of the egg or sperm causes distress and jealousy on the part of the parent of the opposite sex. Often other family members and friends know that the child is the result of donor insemination, and this "secret" may be brought up at some point in the child or adolescent's life. It is best for the parents to be the ones to tell the child about his or her origins. We should also note that the egg or sperm donor, as we know from the news, may have the same issues as other birth parents.

Acknowledgments

Inclusion and exclusion are huge issues in adoption. It is therefore extremely difficult to shorten a list. I will take the time to thank many people, in general and in particular, who have contributed to my life and work in the world of adoption. (Please know that many of you are included in my heart even though space required shortening of lists.)

To all of the birth parents and birth families, especially mine—to my mother, Eileen, who gave me life, and shared with me a great sense of family and of humor; to my brother Dan who searched for me; to my lovely niece, Molly Eileen, who brings me a sense of connection—not only to her—but to my mother, her grandmother; to my brother Kevin and his wife Patricia who know from their hearts about extending family to reach beyond, and to my birth mother's husband who was a very kind and gentle man whom I would have been proud to have as my father. To my nieces Caitlin and Maddie. To other birth parents who have taught me so very much: Linda Phillips Brown, Mina Bicknell, Sheridan Robbins, Susan Darke, Debbie Blanchard, Sophie Gordon, Candace Kunz, Jennie Petersen, Sally Fine, Patricia Kellogg Friedman, Lee Campbell, Fred Greenman, Walter Brown, Charlie Christopher, Lavonne Stiffler, Loren Coleman, Brenda Romanchik, Temple Odom, and to all of the birth families who have sought healing at CFFC or who have taken one of our courses; to all of the birth parents and birth families who know they are missing someone, and to those who don't know, but who, in some way, feel it anyway.

To all of the adoptive parents and extended families, especially mine—to my dearest Mom and Dad, "Sarah" and Danny, and the others from that era who had to do it all on their own, without the help of books and articles and wise ones who came before; to my favorite grandmother, Delia Barry Welch, who came from Ireland at age sixteen and who knew disconnection and loss—she was the storyteller in my family, and we loved each other dearly; to my cousins Debbie and Jeffrey, who have always been my relatives of the heart, and to my cousin Barry, who shared a playpen with me as a toddler and who knows, so well, the importance of connections. To the other adoptive parents and families for whom I have great respect: The Killians, Pappases, Niarhos, Schaners, Pinderhughes/Loomises, Barrios/Hattaways, Sharon Kaplan Roszia, the Salters, Joe and Becky Kroll, Ellen Harris, Eleanor and Jack LeCain, Lynn and Steve Jacobs, Nancy and Tony Erdman, the Capitman/Batts, the Holmes/Jacksons, Lauren Frey, the Lewis family, the Silversteins, the Melinas, the Martinez/Dorners, the Christopher/Hesslops, the Hogan/Donaldsons, the Pelletier/Rutkowskis, the Sprengers, the O'Neils, and all of the other adoptive parents, past and future, and their very extended families. And a special remembrance of Josephine Bay Paul, who was an adoptive mother, and who made this book possible through her generous foundation's grant.

To all of my fellow adopted people: Elena Mendoza, Gladys Kapstein, Fred Bay, B. J. Lifton, Rachel Colberg Parseghian, David Zoffoli, Susan Soon Yeum Cox, Sue Harris, Linda Yellin, Bob Childs, Dr. Robert Anderson, Joe Soll, Sascha and Esme Sprengers, Marcy Axness, Jennifer Eckert, Kate Shamon, Janet Goff, Justin, Yim, Anni and Xavier Hogan Donaldson, Aura and Isaac, Liz, Emily, Jason, Jesse and Rosa, Francesca, Liza Steinberg Triggs, Jake and Chris, Deb Johnson, Shane Salter, Charris, Rosa Staehlin, Peter and Elizabeth, Young and Min, Krisanne, Travis and Ian, Brooks, and Stephanie Mello. If I went on, it would take tomes!

To all of the teachers and mentors of my life: Annette Baran, Reuben Pannor, B. J. Lifton, Bob Kegan, Carol Gilligan, David Kantor, Meredith Kantor, Anne Peretz, Norman Paul, Erik Erikson, George Goethels, Joan Goldsmith, Shango Johnson, Sara Lawrence Lightfoot, Elaine Pinderhughes, and to the Lizard—Wilbury Crockett. Special thanks to my editor, Deanne Urmy, who is compassionate and insightful and has a strong sense of connections.

Finally, to my dearest friends and family who have maintained connection throughout all of my hibernations as I wrote this book. And last, a very special thanks to Seacia, who helped to keep me on course, and to Bailey, the Black Lab, who literally and figuratively was beside me all the way along with Herschel, the Siamese, who kept both my computer and my heart warm.